T0311420

An Analysis of

Martin Luther King Jr.'s

Why We Can't Wait

Jason Xidias

Published by Macat International Ltd
24:13 Coda Centre, 189 Munster Road, London SW6 6AW.

Distributed exclusively by Routledge
2 Park Square, Milton Park, Abingdon, Oxon OX14 4RN
711 Third Avenue, New York, NY 10017, USA

Routledge is an imprint of the Taylor & Francis Group, an informa business

www.macat.com
info@macat.com

Cataloguing in Publication Data
A catalogue record for this book is available from the British Library.
Library of Congress Cataloguing-in-Publication Data is available upon request.
Cover illustration: Capucine Deslouis

ISBN 978-1-912303-33-5 (hardback)
ISBN 978-1-912128-12-9 (paperback)
ISBN 978-1-912282-21-0 (e-book)

Notice
The information in this book is designed to orientate readers of the work under analysis,
to elucidate and contextualise its key ideas and themes, and to aid in the development
of critical thinking skills. It is not meant to be used, nor should it be used, as a
substitute for original thinking or in place of original writing or research. References and
notes are provided for informational purposes and their presence does not constitute
endorsement of the information or opinions therein. This book is presented solely for
educational purposes. It is sold on the understanding that the publisher is not engaged
to provide any scholarly advice. The publisher has made every effort to ensure that
this book is accurate and up-to-date, but makes no warranties or representations with
regard to the completeness or reliability of the information it contains. The information
and the opinions provided herein are not guaranteed or warranted to produce particular
results and may not be suitable for students of every ability. The publisher shall not be
liable for any loss, damage or disruption arising from any errors or omissions, or from
the use of this book, including, but not limited to, special, incidental, consequential or
other damages caused, or alleged to have been caused, directly or indirectly, by the
information contained within.

CONTENTS

THE MACAT LIBRARY

The Macat Library is a series of unique academic explorations of seminal works in the humanities and social sciences – books and papers that have had a significant and widely recognised impact on their disciplines. It has been created to serve as much more than just a summary of what lies between the covers of a great book. It illuminates and explores the influences on, ideas of, and impact of that book. Our goal is to offer a learning resource that encourages critical thinking and fosters a better, deeper understanding of important ideas.

Each publication is divided into three Sections: Influences, Ideas, and Impact. Each Section has four Modules. These explore every important facet of the work, and the responses to it.

This Section-Module structure makes a Macat Library book easy to use, but it has another important feature. Because each Macat book is written to the same format, it is possible (and encouraged!) to cross-reference multiple Macat books along the same lines of inquiry or research. This allows the reader to open up interesting interdisciplinary pathways.

To further aid your reading, lists of glossary terms and people mentioned are included at the end of this book (these are indicated by an asterisk [*] throughout) – as well as a list of works cited.

Macat has worked with the University of Cambridge to identify the elements of critical thinking and understand the ways in which six different skills combine to enable effective thinking.
Three allow us to fully understand a problem; three more give us the tools to solve it. Together, these six skills make up the **PACIER** model of critical thinking. They are:

ANALYSIS – understanding how an argument is built
EVALUATION – exploring the strengths and weaknesses of an argument
INTERPRETATION – understanding issues of meaning

CREATIVE THINKING – coming up with new ideas and fresh connections
PROBLEM-SOLVING – producing strong solutions
REASONING – creating strong arguments

To find out more, visit **WWW.MACAT.COM.**

CRITICAL THINKING AND *WHY WE CAN'T WAIT*

Primary critical thinking skill: REASONING
Secondary critical thinking skill: CREATIVE THINKING

Martin Luther King's policy of non-violent protest in the struggle for civil rights in the United States during the second half of the twentieth century led to fundamental shifts in American government policy relating to segregation, and a cultural shift in the treatment of African Americans.

King's 1964 book *Why We Can't Wait* creates strong, well-structured arguments as to why he and his followers chose to wage a nonviolent struggle in the fight to advance freedom and equality for black people following 'three hundred years of humiliation, abuse, and deprivation.' The author highlights a number of reasons why African Americans must demand their civil rights, including frustration at the lack of political will to tackle racism and inequality. Freedoms gained by African nations after years of colonial rule, as well as the US trumpeting its own values of freedom and equality in an ideological war with the Soviet Union, also played their part.

King dealt with the counter-argument that civil rights for blacks would be detrimental to whites in America by explaining that racism is a disease that deeply penetrates both the white and the black psyche. His reasoning dictated that the brave act of nonviolent mass protest would provoke the kind of thinking that would eventually eliminate racism, and give birth to equality for all of 'God's children.'

ABOUT THE AUTHOR OF THE ORIGINAL WORK

Martin Luther King Jr. was born Michael King in 1929, in Atlanta in the United States. His father was a Baptist pastor, also called Michael King, who changed both their names in 1934 in honor of the sixteenth-century German religious reformer Martin Luther. Deeply devout and highly intelligent, King Jr. gained three degrees, the first of which he received at the age of 19. He led the Civil Rights Movement in America from 1955, and was assassinated on April 4, 1968, in Memphis, Tennessee, at the age of just 39. In the process, Martin Luther King Jr. became a martyr to the causes of racial equality and human rights.

ABOUT THE AUTHOR OF THE ANALYSIS

Dr Jason Xidias holds a PhD in European Politics from King's College London, where he completed a comparative dissertation on immigration and citizenship in Britain and France. He was also a Visiting Fellow in European Politics at the University of California, Berkeley. Currently, he is Lecturer in Political Science at New York University.

ABOUT MACAT

GREAT WORKS FOR CRITICAL THINKING

Macat is focused on making the ideas of the world's great thinkers accessible and comprehensible to everybody, everywhere, in ways that promote the development of enhanced critical thinking skills.

It works with leading academics from the world's top universities to produce new analyses that focus on the ideas and the impact of the most influential works ever written across a wide variety of academic disciplines. Each of the works that sit at the heart of its growing library is an enduring example of great thinking. But by setting them in context – and looking at the influences that shaped their authors, as well as the responses they provoked – Macat encourages readers to look at these classics and game-changers with fresh eyes. Readers learn to think, engage and challenge their ideas, rather than simply accepting them.

WAYS IN TO THE TEXT

KEY POINTS

- Noted as a great public speaker and civil rights leader, Martin Luther King Jr. (1929–68) is one of the most important figures in the history of the United States.

- Published in 1964, *Why We Can't Wait* explains the process and events leading up to the "Negro Revolution"* (King's term for the nonviolent uprising of African Americans against racial discrimination in 1963), and details why African Americans chose to use the method of nonviolence to combat racism and segregation* (the separation of black people and white people in American society).

- *Why We Can't Wait* has been a source of inspiration for many different kinds of political and social movements worldwide.

Who Was Martin Luther King Jr.?

Martin Luther King Jr., the author of *Why We Can't Wait* (1964), is widely recognized as a key figure in American history, noted as one of history's great speakers and for his leadership of the Civil Rights Movement*—the struggle for social and legal equality for black Americans. Born in the city of Atlanta, Georgia, in 1929, King received a BA from Morehouse College in Georgia in 1944, a Bachelor of Divinity from Crozer Theological Seminary in Chester, Pennsylvania, in 1951, and a PhD in Theology from Boston University in 1955.

From a young age, King followed his father's example by showing a strong commitment to Christian morals* (the code of "right" behavior as laid down by Christian communities), civil disobedience* (not complying with laws considered unjust), equality, and peace. A third-generation Baptist* minister, King led the Civil Rights Movement in the United States from 1955. The movement started and thrived in the 1950s and 1960s, when black people in the United States organized themselves in their struggle against discrimination.

King was assassinated in Memphis, Tennessee, in 1968. A petty criminal, James Earl Ray,* confessed to the crime; although he quickly withdrew his confession, Ray was sentenced to 99 years in prison in 1969.

King is remembered for his central role in a number of pivotal moments in the struggle for civil rights in America during this period. He famously led the Montgomery Bus Boycott* of 1955, when African American bus passengers sat in white-only designated areas and refused to give up their seats. He also delivered a speech in the American capital at the end of the 1963 "March on Washington,"* one of the largest political rallies for human rights in American history, calling for an end to racism and inequality in the course of what was to become known as the "I Have a Dream"* speech. Thanks to King's efforts, and those of the activists who fought alongside him, the American government passed the Civil Rights Act of 1964,* which banned discrimination on the grounds of race, and the Voting Rights Act of 1965,* which prohibited racial discrimination in voting.

Today there is a federal holiday in the United States that bears King's name and commemorates his great contributions to advancing equality for African Americans and other minorities.

What Does *Why We Can't Wait* Say?

Why We Can't Wait is a detailed explanation and analysis of the nonviolent social movement against racial segregation that took place in the United States from 1955 to 1963. In particular, King focuses on what he calls the "Negro Revolution" of 1963, a year in which African Americans protested in large numbers against racism and segregation. He describes events leading up to that year, and explains why he and other activists chose the city of Birmingham, Alabama, as the place to start their movement and be the movement's strategic hub. King also explains exactly why he and his followers decided to wage a nonviolent struggle to advance freedom and equality for black people following "three hundred years of humiliation, abuse, and deprivation."[1]

King analyzes the many reasons why the "Negro Revolution" took place at the precise moment it did. He concludes:

- African Americans were deeply frustrated over the lack of political will in the administration of US president John F. Kennedy* to tackle racism and inequality in the wake of the landmark Supreme Court* legal case of *Brown vs. the Board of Education*—a 1954 ruling in which state laws allowing the separation of white and black people in public schools were declared unconstitutional.

- African Americans had been inspired by the recent victories of the people of many African nations in gaining freedom from oppression from the European nations that had colonized them. Black people in the United States saw that their counterparts abroad were gaining independence and holding high-profile positions, such as ministers and heads of state. According to King, African Americans felt a bond with these people, based on a common experience of oppression and a desire to be free.

- The year, 1963, was the 100th anniversary of former US president Abraham Lincoln's* Emancipation Proclamation* of 1863, which required slaves to be freed in all parts of the United States.

- America was involved in an ideological struggle with the Soviet Union (or "USSR"*) at this time. The long period of military tension known as the Cold War* pitted the economic and social systems of the United States and the Soviet Union (democracy and capitalism* in the US, authoritarian communism* in the USSR) against one another. In trying to win the argument about which system was best, the US promoted its belief in freedom and equality as a right for all people in countries around the world—yet King saw that there was still clear segregation and inequality in America itself.

In his book, King describes nonviolent protest as an ethical practice that combats "physical force" (the kind employed by a number of white racists) with "soul force,"[2] based on the moral teachings of the Bible.* Furthermore, he argues that three previous acknowledged civil rights leaders—the activist Booker T. Washington,* the social theorist and activist W. E. B. Du Bois,* and the Jamaican activist Marcus Garvey*—were misguided for different reasons. He believes that Washington was too close to white, southern business interests and was too passive in his demands, while Du Bois was too elitist in his advocacy for a Talented Tenth*—a term he popularized, which describes the idea that one in ten black men would become the leadership class of African Americans. Garvey's belief in black separatism,* meanwhile (basically the idea that black people and white people should form two separate nations), neglected the human need for reconciliation and redemption. King portrays racism as a disease, much like cancer, that deeply penetrates both the white and the black psyche. He argues that nonviolent mass protest would in itself provoke the kind of thinking that would eventually eliminate racism and give birth to equality for all of "God's children."

King makes it clear that he chose Birmingham, Alabama, as the starting point and symbolic core of this nonviolent campaign against racism because it was both the largest industrial city in the South at the time and the most racially segregated. It was a place where African Americans had no civil rights and where the police used dogs and water hoses to terrorize protestors. King firmly believed that if black people could successfully overcome segregation in Birmingham, then they could use the momentum they would gain to do the same at a national level.

On May 10, 1963, King's strategy of nonviolence produced the desired effect as Birmingham's authorities responded to black demonstrations by promising:

- to desegregate the city within 90 days
- to release African Americans who had been jailed for protesting during the campaign
- to open up access to jobs previously denied to black workers
- to engage in further dialogue about racism and inequality.

Why Does *Why We Can't Wait* Matter?

King wrote *Why We Can't Wait* in the spring and summer of 1963 and completed it in early 1964. He published it at a turbulent time in the US, when President John F. Kennedy had been assassinated and subsequently replaced by his vice president, Lyndon Baines Johnson.* King wanted to build on the momentum he had gained from his March on Washington, and the impact of his "I Have a Dream" speech. The timing of the book was crucial, because legislation aimed at advancing the civil rights cause had stalled in the lawmaking body of government known as Congress* after Kennedy's death, with many white people claiming that lawmaking in this area was unnecessary and criticizing black people for asking for too much.

King and his followers were determined to advance this legislation through Congress by highlighting America's history of racial discrimination and the everyday realities of discrimination and segregation in the country. They were also determined to present the moral philosophy behind their nonviolent resistance movement. They wanted to create much greater public consciousness of the issues at stake and to attract even more attention to widespread racism and inequality in America. The book was just one of a number of elements that helped King achieve his goals. Congress passed the Civil Rights Act and the Voting Rights Act in 1964 and 1965 respectively.

Why We Can't Wait was clearly a response to the conditions of the times, a determined effort to combat segregation and to highlight the Kennedy administration's lack of political will to tackle both racism and inequality. But King's ideas about nonviolent resistance, the way he applied them, and his insistent struggle for social justice all remain a great source of inspiration for activists today.

Yet King felt the problems of American society went beyond racism toward African Americans. He believed that many groups were oppressed (women and Native Americans, for example) and he was certain a radical restructuring of society was needed for there to be true social justice. So *Why We Can't Wait* was more than just a plea for equal legal rights. As King himself put it: "It is forcing America to face all its interrelated flaws—racism, poverty, militarism and materialism."[3]

Today, Martin Luther King Jr. is seen as a symbol of freedom, justice, equality, and peace. He is the only person with a federal holiday dedicated to his honor in the United States who did not hold the office of president. His Christian vision for American society emphasized that what comes after violence has always been bitterness, but that nonviolence provokes a sense of shame among those who oppress others; sooner or later, what comes after nonviolence is reconciliation and redemption. As long as there is injustice in the world, these ideas will still demand to be heard.

NOTES

1   Martin Luther King Jr., *Why We Can't Wait* (New York: Penguin, 2000), 3.

2   Martin Luther King Jr., "I Have a Dream" speech, August 28, 1963.

3   Martin Luther King Jr., "A Testament of Hope," in *A Testament of Hope: The Essential Writings of Martin Luther King Jr.*, ed. James M. Washington (New York: Harper & Row, 1986), 315.

SECTION 1
INFLUENCES

MODULE 1
THE AUTHOR AND THE
HISTORICAL CONTEXT

KEY POINTS

- Martin Luther King Jr., a brilliant orator and a leader of the American Civil Rights Movement,* was one of the greatest figures in American history.

- *Why We Can't Wait* explains the history of racism in America and the immoral nature of racism and segregation,* and provides detailed arguments for why African Americans should be granted equal legal rights immediately.

- King wrote the text at a crucial time in American history: racism, segregation, and economic inequality were major problems; civil rights legislation was stalled after President John F. Kennedy's* assassination; and it was the 100-year anniversary of the Emancipation Proclamation* (the legislation that freed American slaves).

Why Read this Text?

Martin Luther King Jr.'s *Why We Can't Wait* (1964) provides a detailed account of the history of racism toward African Americans in the United States, the process and events leading up to the uprising King described as the "Negro Revolution"* of 1963, and the Civil Rights Movement more broadly. The text also justifies why he and his followers chose to use nonviolent means to combat discrimination and segregation while providing essential insight into the realities and complexities of the time and explaining why racism is morally wrong; for King, racism and material greed are inherently linked.

King goes on to detail how he and other activists went about

> **❝** I believe that unarmed truth and unconditional love will have the final word in reality. This is why right, temporarily defeated, is stronger than evil triumphant. **❞**
>
> Martin Luther King Jr., Nobel Peace Prize speech, December 10, 1964

organizing a nonviolent social movement, and why we must always use love to combat hatred. He argues that resisting discrimination of all kinds is a moral duty and doing so peacefully displays great inner strength and courage; unlike violence, this will ultimately lead to greater reflection, reconciliation between the oppressor and the oppressed, and redemption of the human soul. Today, the text continues to serve as both a guide and inspiration for certain activists who struggle against racism and inequality, and who call for radical economic and social transformations in society in order to reach a higher level of humanity.

The text was both a crucial contribution to the Civil Rights Movement and a seminal work in the disciplines of history, sociology, and political science.

Author's Life

Martin Luther King Jr. was born Michael King in Atlanta, Georgia, in 1929. His father changed his son's name to glorify the German religious leader Martin Luther* following a family pilgrimage to Germany in 1934; the first Martin Luther was instrumental in the founding of the modern Protestant branch of Christianity following the schism with the Roman Catholic Church known as the "Reformation" in the sixteenth century.

King was a bright student who especially enjoyed choir and debating. He skipped two grades in high school and, upon passing an entrance exam, started university at Morehouse College in Atlanta in 1944 at the age of 15, where he received a Bachelor of Arts in 1948.

King went on to receive a Bachelor of Divinity from Crozer Theological Seminary in Chester, Pennsylvania, in 1951, as well as a PhD in Theology from Boston University in 1955.

While King was completing his doctoral dissertation, he met his wife Coretta Scott* at the New England Conservatory of Music. They had four children together. In 1954, just before he finished his PhD, he became minister at the Dexter Avenue Baptist Church in Montgomery, Alabama; both his grandfather and father had also been Protestant ministers.

Like his father, King also became a social activist, struggling against racism and inequality. In 1955, at the age of 26, King led the Montgomery Bus Boycott,* an event in which African Americans refused to ride the city's buses in protest at segregated seating. Due to media coverage, from that point onward, King became much more widely known as the leader of the Civil Rights Movement and a champion of social equality. He gained further notoriety in 1963 leading his famous March on Washington,* delivering what is widely considered to be one of the great speeches in history: "I Have a Dream."* The next year he received the Nobel Peace Prize for improving humanity through nonviolent protest. In 1968, at the age of 39, he was assassinated—allegedly by the criminal James Earl Ray,* who confessed and then withdrew his confession—in Memphis, Tennessee. The nature of the murder remains controversial to some.

Author's Background

Although the highest court in the United States, the Supreme Court,* had ruled in 1954 that all states must end segregation in public schools (the landmark *Brown vs. the Board of Education** case), in 1963, most southern schools were still segregated. Both the Democrats* and the Republicans* (the two largest political parties in the United States) had promised to address racism in their campaign manifestos, but had failed to do so in practice—something true, also, of the administration of President John F. Kennedy, which from 1961 to 1963 largely turned a blind eye to the issue. Growing frustration over this reality, added to the facts that more than 30 African nations had gained independence from colonial rule and that 1963 was the centennial of Abraham Lincoln's* Emancipation Proclamation, freeing US slaves, made the year significant for those struggling for civil rights. The "Negro Revolution," as King called it, built on previous nonviolent resistance, including the important Montgomery Bus Boycott of 1955,* which began four days after Rosa Parks,* an African American woman, refused to give up her seat for a white man and was subsequently arrested and fined. These developments aimed to pressure government to pass civil rights legislation that would outlaw segregation in practice and eliminate discriminatory measures at the level of states, which effectively prevented African Americans from casting their vote in elections—even though the Fifteenth Amendment to the US Constitution, passed in 1870, gave them the right to do so. These discriminatory measures included poll taxes* (a tax required to vote) and literacy tests* (tests measuring reading and writing skills, which discriminated against those denied a decent education—notably black people).

Ironically, these developments took place against the backdrop of the Cold War*—a long period of ideologically fueled global tension in which the United States sought to champion itself as a bastion of freedom and equality to the world.

MODULE 2
ACADEMIC CONTEXT

KEY POINTS

- In *Why We Can't Wait*, Martin Luther King Jr. argues that nonviolent protest is a correct and necessary form of conflict to achieve reconciliation and redemption—what he calls a "beloved community,"1 in which white people and black people live side by side in equality.

- King's understanding and use of nonviolent protest is based on the teachings of the Bible and the ideas of the philosopher Josiah Royce,* the author Henry David Thoreau,* and the Indian political leader Mohandas Karmachand "Mahatma" Gandhi.*

- King's doctrine of nonviolent resistance continues to be a powerful source of inspiration for social activists worldwide.

The Work In Its Context

In *Why We Can't Wait*, Martin Luther King Jr. combined the biblical doctrines of "turning the other cheek" and "loving thy enemy" (which come from the Sermon on the Mount and the Sermon on the Plain in the New Testament) with the teachings of previous advocates of civil disobedience* (the idea that it is one's moral duty to oppose injustice through action such as refusing to observe certain laws, for example), and his own intolerance for racial discrimination. From this, his conception of nonviolent resistance developed as a means by which individuals could unite together to struggle for reform, reconciliation, and redemption. This meant that African Americans would turn to historical examples and moral arguments and protest to make racist individuals reflect on and reconsider their words and actions. King's

> ❝ The words 'bad timing' came to be ghosts haunting our every move in Birmingham. Yet people who used this argument were ignorant of the background of our planning ... they did not realize that it was ridiculous to speak of timing when the clock of history showed that the Negro had already suffered one hundred years of delay. ❞
>
> Martin Luther King Jr., *Why We Can't Wait*

ultimate objective was to create a "beloved community," in which white people and black people could live together in harmony and equality.

King's philosophy was also grounded in the biblical idea that redemption would not come before suffering. As he put it, "My Bible tells me that Good Friday comes before Easter."[1] For him, setbacks were an inevitable part of the process, and they must be learned from and overcome. King was also motivated by the teachings of Christian saints whose ideas shaped his approach of using love against hatred at all times, everywhere. In his last speech in April 1968, the day before his assassination, he assumed that becoming a martyr was imminent, stating:"I may not get there with you ... but we, as a people, will get to the Promised Land."[2]

Overview of the Field

The first scholar to define and use the concept of civil disobedience was the American thinker Henry David Thoreau in his work *Civil Disobedience* (1849). In his opposition to the institution of slavery in the United States and the Mexican–American War* (a war in which the issue of slavery loomed large), he argued that it was a moral and civic duty to protest against unjust laws, whatever the consequences. In making this argument, Thoreau recounts his own personal experience of refusing to pay a poll tax,* and consequently being temporarily imprisoned. His ideas were rooted in the Christian notion of moral conviction, and he prioritized this over government-made laws.

Mohandas Karmachand Gandhi developed the concept of civil disobedience further in the twentieth century and translated it into mass social movements. Gandhi first used peaceful protest against the discrimination of Asians and black Africans in South Africa; then, back home in India, he developed the doctrine of *Satyagraha** (literally, "love-force"), which consisted of a combination of marches, hunger and worker strikes, and boycotts in protest at the injustices of British colonial rule. He also empathized with the discrimination suffered by African Americans through his articles in *The Crisis*, the magazine of the US activist organization the National Association for the Advancement of Colored People (NAACP).*

Gandhi's ultimate goal was to make the British face up to the facts of injustice and to pressure them to negotiate as equals. He saw violence as an act that separates people and causes bitterness, and nonviolence as a communal exercise that strives for reconciliation and redemption. As he put it, "To me, Truth is God and there is no way to find Truth except the way of nonviolence."[3] Gandhi's doctrine provided the philosophical context for King's nonviolent campaign from 1955 until his assassination in 1968.

Academic Influences

Martin Luther King Jr. was a third-generation Baptist minister. At Boston University, where he gained his PhD, he came into contact with the work of the philosopher Josiah Royce. Reading his *The Problem of Christianity* (1913), King was captivated by Royce's concept of a "beloved community." This was an idea grounded in the notion that an entire community accepts the hardships of history, and intuitively feels that words and actions that affect certain members of that community—racism in this case—affect everyone. By this he did not mean the utopian* image of the Peaceable Kingdom,* a place described in the Bible in which lions and lambs coexisted in perfect harmony; rather, it was a situation in which people with differences could come together as equals and reconcile themselves in order to achieve redemption and peace. In this beloved community, love triumphs over hate, peace over war, and brotherhood over evils such as racism, hunger, poverty, and homelessness. Just as suffering was part of the path to redemption in the Bible, for King, conflict and its resolution were inevitable parts of striving for, and reaching, a higher level of humanity.

To achieve this, King believed that there was a need for all of society to adopt a doctrine of nonviolence—a concept that Henry David Thoreau originally theorized. While a student at Crozer Theological Seminary, King also studied the teachings of Mohandas Karmachand Gandhi, who had developed Thoreau's concept of civil disobedience further in the context of racism in South Africa and India's resistance to British colonialism. Gandhi's commitment to transforming love into a powerful force for social change impressed King, and he adopted a similar vision in his struggle to advance the cause of African Americans. The first time he put this into practice was at the Montgomery Bus Boycott* of 1955. Despite putting his life in danger he chose not to use armed bodyguards, and he reacted to the subsequent bombing of his home with compassion, reiterating the biblical notion of loving one's enemies.

King understood nonviolence as a way of life, open to everyone, everywhere. As he put it, nonviolence is the "guiding light of our movement. [Jesus] Christ* furnished the spirit and motivation and Gandhi furnished the method."[4]

NOTES

1   Martin Luther King Jr., "Why I am opposed to the war in Vietnam" sermon,
     Riverside Church, New York, April, 30, 1967.

2   Martin Luther King Jr., "I've been to the mountaintop" sermon, Memphis,
     Tennessee, April 3, 1968.

3   Mohandas Karmachand Gandhi, "Speech, December 20, 1926," in Gandhi,
     Gandhi: All Men Are Brothers, ed. Krishna Kripalani (New York: Continuum
     International Publishing Group, 2011).

4   Clayborne Carson, ed., *The Papers of Martin Luther King Jr.*, Vol. V (Berkeley
     and Los Angeles: University of California Press, 2005), 423.

MODULE 3
THE PROBLEM

KEY POINTS

- *Why We Can't Wait* details the process and events that led up to the "Negro Revolution"* of 1963 and the importance of Birmingham, Alabama. Furthermore, it explains why African Americans chose to use nonviolent resistance, rather than violence, to combat racism and inequality.

- King presents his argument in eight chapters that explore the "Negro Revolution," racism, and resistance in Birmingham, and what he and his fellow activists hope to accomplish in "the days to come."

- King firmly believes that nonviolent resistance will provoke reflection, reform, reconciliation, and redemption—a situation in which white people and black people overcome conflict and live together in harmony and equality.

Core Question

In *Why We Can't Wait*, Martin Luther King Jr. asks three questions: Why did African Americans revolt in 1963? Why did they choose Birmingham, Alabama, as the strategic core of their protest? And, finally, why did they choose nonviolent resistance instead of violent revolution?

The first question addresses the cumulative effects of racism from the period of slavery to 1963.

Slavery disrupted every aspect of human freedom and dignity: it prevented free speech, it separated families, and punished workers for "disobedience." Furthermore, although black struggles led to some advances in freedom and rights during the era of Reconstruction* (the period between 1865 and 1877 in which the Southern states

> **❝** Injustice anywhere is a threat to justice everywhere. We are caught in an inescapable network of mutuality, tied in a single garment of destiny. Whatever affects one directly, affects all indirectly. **❞**
>
> Martin Luther King Jr., *Why We Can't Wait*

were reincorporated into the union following the American Civil War* between the Northern and the Southern states), discrimination and violence subsequently disenfranchised* black people during the period of the "Jim Crow"* laws (laws passed with the intention of segregating black and white Americans, operating in parts of the United States until the 1960s). King describes the liberation of 1963: "Just as lightening makes no sound until it strikes, the Negro Revolution generated quietly. But when it struck, the revealing flash of its power and the impact of sincerity and fervor displayed a force of frightening intensity. Three hundred years of humiliation, abuse, and deprivation cannot be expected to find voice in a whisper."[1]

The second question focuses on why King and his fellow activists chose Birmingham, Alabama, as the starting point and strategic core of the nonviolent protest movement. In this section, King explores the economic and racist authoritative structure of the city, arguing that the conditions of black people were worse there than anywhere else in the country, despite the fact that Birmingham was an industrial city where many white people were gaining social mobility* (the ability to better one's social status through factors such as prosperity). King argued that if African Americans were successful in overcoming injustice in Birmingham, this would serve as a stepping-stone for achieving the same at a national level.

Finally, King describes the art of nonviolent protest, and explains why African Americans were using this strategy to combat racism. He claims that "soul force" (that is, challenging hatred with love) is the best means of constructing an American democracy based on the founding principles of the nation: liberty, equality, and brotherhood. Furthermore, the violent way in which white people responded to nonviolent protests revealed the full brutality of the problem to the world, which, in turn, provoked shame, compassion, and support.

The Participants

As a well-respected Baptist minister and brilliant orator, King was well positioned to lead social activists in their struggle against racism and segregation in the United States. King gained notoriety for his boldness and courageousness in the Montgomery Bus Boycott* of 1955, and later in his March on Washington* in 1963, where he delivered his famous "I Have a Dream"* speech.

King organized activists and trained them in nonviolent resistance. These followers were instructed to spread the teachings of Jesus Christ,* in particular, to use love against hatred at all times to achieve reflection, reconciliation, and redemption. Two key figures in the resistance movement were Reverend Wyatt Walker,* who secretly traveled throughout Birmingham establishing the logistics of where demonstrations would take place, and Reverend Fred Shuttlesworth,* who organized the Alabama Christian Movement for Human Rights (ACHR)* and was determined to end "the terrorist, racist rule of Bull Connor,* Birmingham's Commissioner of Public Safety."[2]

Bull Connor was a powerful city commissioner in Birmingham, Alabama, and one of the major enemies of the movement. He ruled over municipal affairs, was deeply racist, and "prided himself on knowing how to handle the Negro and keep him in his 'place.'"[3] He was a key voice in an authoritative structure that segregated all areas of society and used scare tactics and injunctions*—legal means—to prevent associations such as the National Association for the Advancement of Colored People (NAACP)* from protesting.

Finally, King and his followers pressured the administration of

President John F. Kennedy* to pass civil rights legislation to end segregation and ensure equal voting rights for all black people.

The Contemporary Debate

Martin Luther King Jr. and his followers were challenging all individuals who sought to perpetuate racism and safeguard segregation. Connor was among these, but so was the governor of Alabama, George Wallace.* In Wallace's 1963 inaugural address, he promised to prevent the federal government from desegregating public institutions in the state, shouting, "Segregation now, segregation tomorrow, segregation forever."[4] Subsequently, this became a rallying cry for many who opposed King and the Civil Rights Movement.*

King directly confronted this advocacy for prolonged segregation by delivering persuasive speeches that criticized racists' arguments as baseless. The most famous of these took place on August 28, 1963, following the March on Washington, when over 200,000 people assembled in the nation's capital to listen to King's "I Have a Dream" speech. King linked black civil rights aspirations with the founding principles of the American Republic—the inalienable rights of life, liberty, and the pursuit of happiness—and called for greater democracy. These speeches, coupled with popular protest, pressured Lyndon Baines Johnson* (president of the United States following the assassination of John F. Kennedy) to introduce legislation that later became the Voting Rights Act of 1965.*

NOTES

1 Martin Luther King Jr., *Why We Can't Wait* (New York: Penguin, 2000), 3.

2 King, *Why We Can't Wait*, 49.

3 King, *Why We Can't Wait*, 47.

4 George Wallace, "Inaugural address," Montgomery, Alabama, January 14, 1963.

MODULE 4
THE AUTHOR'S CONTRIBUTION

KEY POINTS

- *Why We Can't Wait* contributes to our understanding of the history of racism and segregation* in America, and the effort of African Americans to overcome this between the mid-1950s and 1963.

- King built on the ideas of previous African American leaders and on the concept of civil disobedience* theorized and practiced by both the US author Henry David Thoreau* and the Indian liberation leader Mohandas Karmachand Gandhi * to show how nonviolent resistance could overcome racism and segregation in America.

- King published his analysis of the process and events leading up to the "Negro Revolution"* of 1963, and the conditions African Americans faced, at a crucial point in history, when civil rights legislation was stalled in Congress* following the assassination of President John F. Kennedy.*

Author's Aims

Martin Luther King Jr.'s *Why We Can't Wait* has several aims. First, King seeks to express in detail the extent to which Birmingham, Alabama, is a racist and racially segregated city. Second, he shows how Birmingham could serve as an example of hope and progress for the rest of the country, if he and his followers are able to overturn segregation there. Third, King aims to demonstrate the cumulative effects of racism over three centuries in the United States and how 1963, being the centennial of President Abraham Lincoln's* Emancipation Proclamation* (the edict that America's slaves should be freed), is a crucial moment for African Americans to work together to radically

> ❝ We must come to see that the end we seek is a society at peace with itself, a society that can live with its conscience. ❞
>
> Martin Luther King Jr., *Why We Can't Wait*

transform society for the better. Fourth, he offers his readers details about the art of nonviolent resistance, and explains why this is the best strategy for African Americans to overcome racism and segregation.

King's overall aim is to show that despite the fact that America has had a very violent past of slavery, racism, and segregation, he believes that one day all Americans can be reconciled, and the nation's soul can be redeemed. To achieve this, white oppressors must deeply reflect on past and present injustices, experience shame, and ultimately recognize black people as equal members of society. As Gandhi put it years earlier: "Through our pain we will make them see their injustice."[1] That being said, King makes clear that white people can't be described as a single entity. There are those who actively oppress black people, those who try to do moral good but are intimidated to maintain the status quo, and those who remain silent. He finds all of these people at fault. In this sense, the revolution was not just about mobilizing those with strong moral convictions but also inspiring the silent to come forward and to stop supporting a system that they know to be oppressive.

Practically speaking, King sought to convince the administrations of presidents John F. Kennedy and Lyndon Baines Johnson* to pass federal legislation that would desegregate public institutions and ensure black people have equal voting rights.

Approach
King begins the book by comparing the lives of two African American children—a boy living in Harlem, New York, and a girl living in

Birmingham, Alabama. While these are two very different places, both children have many things in common: they live in poverty, face great discrimination, and have very difficult futures ahead of them. This analogy shows that although many portray racism as a problem of the South, it was in reality a national problem. In the North, racism might have been subtle, but it was equally unjust and had dire consequences for the black people that reside there.

King makes it clear that not only does racism have a detrimental effect on the identity and lives of African Americans; it is also damaging for white people, who have to live with the legacy of slavery and a racist conscience. King goes on to show how, in Birmingham, segregation has ill effects on the quality of life of the entire community. For example, instead of desegregating public parks, as stipulated by a state court order, public officials chose to close them.

Yet, despite this gloomy picture at the start of the book, the introduction ends with a sense of hope, as both the boy and the girl have great faith and believe that they will one day overcome their difficult conditions.

From this analogy, King proceeds to detail the long history of oppression endured by African Americans, and he expresses his belief that, if they unite in mass, nonviolent resistance, they can achieve reconciliation with white people, and all of American society can live side by side in a state of equality.

Contribution in Context

King's analysis of racism in America, and the manner in which it might be overcome, builds on the work of previous African American leaders. One such figure was Frederick Douglass,* who escaped from slavery and became a social reformer, public speaker, and influential writer. He led the abolitionist* movement (the movement to end slavery) and played a key role in shaping Abraham Lincoln's Emancipation Proclamation 100 years earlier in 1863. During the course of his lifetime, Douglass wrote three autobiographies that described racism in America and called for a mass, black struggle against it.

King also builds on the work of the thinker W. E. B. Du Bois,* the first African American to attend Harvard University, who went on to become an influential teacher, researcher, journalist, and activist. Throughout his life, Du Bois exposed the material causes of racism in the United States, and elsewhere, and explained the effects of discrimination on black identity. He continually emphasized the need to overcome racism in order to achieve real democracy.

By drawing on the ideas of these great black leaders, and simultaneously extending the concept of civil disobedience as theorized and practiced by Henry David Thoreau and Mohandas Karmachand "Mahatma" Gandhi (the principle that laws considered unjust should be deliberately contravened), King made an enormous contribution to our understanding of racism in American society, and how African Americans combated it in the hopes of reaching a higher level of humanity.

NOTES

1   Mohandas Karmachand Gandhi, "Speech on nonviolence," September 11, 1906.

SECTION 2
IDEAS

MODULE 5
MAIN IDEAS

KEY POINTS

- The main idea of the text is that African Americans have faced three centuries of racism and inequality, and a mass, nonviolent resistance movement is necessary to overcome this.

- King and his followers chose Birmingham, Alabama, as the starting point and strategic core of their nonviolent movement because it was the most racist and segregated* city in the South.

- King presents his main argument in eight detailed chapters that cover the history of slavery, racism, and segregation in the United States, and explains why civil disobedience* and nonviolence are necessary to overcome injustice and achieve greater democracy.

Key Themes

The core themes of Martin Luther King Jr.'s *Why We Can't Wait* are the legacy of slavery, racism, segregation, civil disobedience, and nonviolence.

King starts by describing slavery as an immoral practice that has had a massive impact on American democracy. He then explains that escaped slaves, together with white radicals, took full advantage of Southern secession (the withdrawal of a territory from a larger national body) to strike a fatal blow to slavery. He then focuses on the failure of Reconstruction* (the period following the American Civil War,* when the United States rebuilt its political structures) and how the racism and violence of the Jim Crow* laws—laws cementing racial segregation—have crippled freedom and equality in America

> **❝** Darkness cannot drive out darkness, only light can do
> that. Hate cannot drive out hate, only love can do that. **❞**
> Martin Luther King Jr., *Strength to Love* (1963)

for nearly a century.

King goes on to describe segregation as an immoral act that ignores the need for reconciliation and redemption. For him, white people and black people need to live alongside one another, overcome their tensions, and construct true freedom and equality together. By doing this, America could redeem itself and become a great democracy.

Finally, King argues that civil disobedience is the best way for black people to achieve freedom and equality. He believes that individuals have the moral and civic duty to oppose unjust laws that degrade humanity. Specifically, King advocates nonviolence as a means by which African Americans can provoke great reflection among white people, cause deep moral shame, and shape progressive change for society at large.

Exploring the Ideas

King first describes slavery as an immoral practice linked to economics, and remembers the black struggles of the past: "Our forebears labored without wages. They made cotton 'king.' And yet out of a bottomless vitality, they continued to thrive and develop. If the cruelties of slavery could not stop us, the opposition we now face will surely fail … Because the goal of America is freedom. Abused and scorned though we may be, our destiny is tied up with America's destiny."[1]

King then describes how in spite of the Emancipation Proclamation* (1863), which promised freedom and equality to African Americans, Jim Crow laws crippled their progress for nearly a century. King then states that America has had three revolutions in its history: its struggle for independence against Great Britain, its Civil

War, and the "Negro Revolution"* of 1963. He focuses his attention on the latter. King describes 1963 as the most important moment of progress since Reconstruction. Civil unrest erupted in nearly one thousand cities across the country, and the potential for great violence lurked below the surface. African Americans saw the streets as the battleground for radical reform, and the motivation for their frustrations was three hundred years of cumulative racial discrimination and inequality.

Although the Supreme Court* decision *Brown vs. the Board of Education** called for the desegregation of public schools, by 1963 only minimal progress had been made in this direction, and racism remained widespread. King considered segregation to be an immoral act that had serious effects on both black people and white people; it prevented interaction and reconciliation between them and, furthermore, did not allow for white people to redeem their past sins of slavery and oppression.

To achieve reconciliation and redemption, conflict was necessary. Drawing from the teachings of Henry David Thoreau* and Mohandas Karmachand "Mahatma" Gandhi,* King firmly believed that civil disobedience was the answer. In other words, black people must disobey the unjust practices of segregation, even if that meant imprisonment or death. In doing this, he called upon black people everywhere to spread love, and engage in nonviolent demonstrations, which, he believed, would cause great reflection, attract great attention, provoke great shame, and ultimately force white people to make concessions. As he puts it: "We know through painful experience that freedom is never voluntarily given by the oppressor; it must be demanded by the oppressed."[2] King and his fellow activists chose Birmingham, Alabama, as a starting point for this process because, in his eyes, it was the most racist city in the country.

Language and Expression

King was one of the most powerful writers and orators in American history. His "Letter from the Birmingham Jail," which forms one section of the book, is a great example. In it, he calmly and persuasively addresses white clergymen. He methodically acknowledges their concerns against the timing and actions of his civil rights campaign in Birmingham. In doing so, he states: "It is unfortunate that demonstrations are taking place … but it is even more unfortunate that the city's white power structure left the Negro community with no alternative."[3] He highlights that, regarding timing, African Americans have been patiently waiting for America to deliver on its promises of freedom and equality since the country's foundation.

·King then uses references to America's Declaration of Independence* of 1776 (the announcement that the young United States considered itself independent from the British Empire) and describes nonviolence as a necessary means of advancing American democracy. Without it, and the reflection and attention it provokes, he argues that white people would never voluntarily give up their power and privileges.

Throughout the text, in addressing white clergymen and racist public officials in Birmingham, King uses a strong moral and prophetic tone: "I am in Birmingham because injustice is here. Just as the prophets of the eighth century B.C. left their villages and carried their 'thus saith the Lord' far beyond the boundaries of their home towns, so am I compelled to carry the gospel of freedom beyond my own home town."[4]

This combination of biblical allusion, strong factual arguments, and calls for America to fulfill the promises of its founding fathers makes for a very powerful argument. Together with demonstrations, this forced concessions from public officials in Birmingham, and shaped progressive change at a national level.

NOTES

1   Martin Luther King Jr., *Why We Can't Wait* (New York: Penguin, 2009), 109.

2   King, *Why We Can't Wait*, 91.

3   King, *Why We Can't Wait*, 87.

4   King, *Why We Can't Wait*, 86.

MODULE 6
SECONDARY IDEAS

KEY POINTS

- The most important secondary idea is the connection King draws between economics and racism; for him, material greed is the driving force behind discrimination and segregation.*

- In *Why We Can't Wait*, King touches on the link between economics and racism; in his later work, he covers this much more thoroughly.

- King believes that following the victory of the nonviolent resistance movement against racism in Birmingham, a broad alliance of oppressed peoples is needed in order to achieve further progress and greater democracy in America.

Other Ideas

Two important secondary themes in Martin Luther King Jr.'s *Why We Can't Wait* are the relationship between economics and racism, and the complicity of white people in furthering segregation.

Since the German economist and political philosopher Karl Marx,* many scholars had addressed the relationship between economics and racism. W. E. B. Du Bois's* *The Souls of Black Folk* (1903) and *Black Reconstruction in America* (1935), for example, were important sources of inspiration for King. While the two had somewhat different visions of how black people should seek to progress in American society, King commemorated Du Bois's contributions and influence in significant detail in his address at Carnegie Hall in New York on February 23, 1968. Du Bois argued that material greed was responsible for racism in America. He showed

❆ The curse of poverty has no justification in our age. It is socially as cruel and blind as the practice of cannibalism at the dawn of civilization, when men ate each other because they had not yet learned to take food from the soil or to consume the abundant animal life around them. The time has come for us to civilize ourselves by the total, direct and immediate abolition of poverty. ❇

Martin Luther King Jr., *Where Do We Go From Here?* (1967)

how white property owners in the South sought to protect their power and privileges by exploiting black labor, and used racism as a tool to attempt to turn poor white people against poor black people so that they would not revolt together against a system that exploited both.

Although white racists were largely responsible for prolonging segregation, King also blames the complicity of all white people who did nothing in practice to overcome it. This includes white clergymen, some of whom argued against the timing and actions of his nonviolent campaign.

Exploring the Ideas

Du Bois's *Black Reconstruction in America* was a Marxist analysis of the link between economics and racism. Its influence on King was considerable, both in 1963 and in his later campaigns against poverty and the Vietnam War* (a bloody conflict in which the United States interceded between 1965 and 1972 hoping to defeat the forces of communist* North Vietnam). Du Bois makes it clear that America became a great economy because of slavery and low-cost wage labor, and that many white people used racism as a tool to justify their exploitation of black people, and also turn poor white people against poor black people rather than against the oppressive system at large.

In *Why We Can't Wait*, King links America's history of slavery and low-cost wage labor to its agricultural and industrial booms of the nineteenth and twentieth centuries. He goes on to point out that, despite the Emancipation Proclamation* and the gains made during Reconstruction,* in 1963 the average median salary of African American workers was only half that of white people, and black people were two and half times more likely to be unemployed. In making this point, he argues that blatantly racist public officials such as Bull Connor* and governor George Wallace* are not the only ones responsible; he also criticizes the actions of all white people complicit in sustaining exploitation and segregation. "Many white Americans of good will have never connected bigotry with economic exploitation. They have deplored prejudice, but tolerated or ignored economic injustice. But the Negro knows that these two evils have a malignant kinship."[1]

Finally, King makes it clear that public officials in Birmingham ultimately made concessions to African Americans primarily because they were concerned at the cost of protests and work stoppages.

Overlooked

The last quarter of the book has received much less attention than the first three-quarters. In the later sections, King looks ahead at the challenging days to come, and transmits a deepening understanding of how the economic and social system of capitalism* sows divisions within the working class, and provides insight on what must be done to overcome this. King makes it evident that white public officials have used the ideology of "different races" to encourage poor southern white people to see themselves as different from poor southern black people because of skin color; however, in reality, all of these individuals are victims of material greed and exploitation. His view is that, if they worked together, they could compel authorities to radically transform society for the better: "The long-standing racist ideology has corrupted and diminished our democratic ideals."[2] King then argues that, in order to assure that democracy will move forward beyond the victory in Birmingham, "the Negro freedom movement will need to secure and extend its alliances with like-minded groups in the larger community."[3]

This emphasis in the last quarter of the book on the link between capitalism and racism, and the need for different oppressed workers to come together, has been overlooked in subsequent literature. While King is normally associated quite narrowly with the Civil Rights Movements,* from 1963 onward he became more radical in his outlook, as highlighted by his efforts to combat poverty and oppose America's foreign policy in Vietnam. For example, in his 1967 speech "Where do we go from here?," King asked: "Why are there forty million poor people in America? … When you begin to ask that question, you are raising a question about the economic system, about a broader distribution of wealth. When you ask that question, you begin to question the capitalist economy … When you deal with this you begin to ask the question 'Who owns the oil?' … 'Who owns the iron ore?'…

'Why is it that people pay water bills in a world that's two-thirds water?'"[4]

NOTES

1 Martin Luther King Jr., *Why We Can't Wait* (New York: Penguin, 2009), 13.

2 King Jr., *Why We Can't Wait*, 147.

3 King Jr., *Why We Can't Wait*, 175.

4 Martin Luther King Jr., "Where do we go from here?" speech, Southern Christian Leadership Conference, Atlanta, Georgia, August 16, 1967.

MODULE 7
ACHIEVEMENT

KEY POINTS

- From 1955 until his assassination in 1968, Martin Luther King Jr. waged a nonviolent struggle against racism, pressuring the US government to pass a series of Civil Rights acts.*

- Several factors enabled this accomplishment, including a deep frustration over the false promises of the government to desegregate public institutions and the centennial of the Emancipation Proclamation* of President Abraham Lincoln.*

- The most important factor limiting King's achievement was the resistance of white racists, who maintained the ideology and practice of racism.

Assessing The Argument

Martin Luther King Jr.'s *Why We Can't Wait* provides an in-depth analysis of the process and key events leading up to the "Negro Revolution"* of 1963.The text explains why the uprising occurred at the time it did, what the implications of it were for African Americans, the results of the movement, and the prospects for further progress.

Building on the work of the US writer Henry David Thoreau,* the Indian political leader Mohandas Karmachand "Mahatma" Gandhi,* and others, King emphasizes that some laws are unjust and have to be confronted with nonviolent resistance. King successfully organized sit-ins, boycotts, and marches that provoked much reflection among white people, and eventually major concessions from public officials in Birmingham, Alabama. This was part of King's broader philosophy that nonviolent conflict was essential in order to achieve

> 66 Human progress never rolls in on wheels of inevitability; it comes through the tireless efforts of men willing to work to be co-workers with God, and without this hard work, time itself becomes an ally of the forces of social stagnation. 99
>
> Martin Luther King Jr., *Why We Can't Wait*

reconciliation and redemption in American society. White people would have to acknowledge the country's dark history of slavery and the oppression of the Jim Crow* era, and carry out radical reforms to address three centuries of racial discrimination and inequality. If this occurred, white and black people would be able to live together peacefully as equal members of society, and white people would be cured of their deep moral burden.

King's philosophy and work has served as a foundation, in conjunction with the nonviolence promoted by Gandhi and others, for progressive social movements worldwide.

Achievement in Context

Civil disobedience* is a central concept in political philosophy, and a practical principle for the advancement of society. Though it has its roots in ancient Greece, it was first theorized and practiced by Thoreau in his famous essay "Civil Disobedience," (1849) and it has since been used in major global developments ranging from Gandhi's opposition to British colonial rule in India to the South African political leader Nelson Mandela's* struggle against the racist regime of South Africa, in which the apartheid* system enshrined segregation* in a systematic, legal fashion.

Nonviolent resistance is a form of civil disobedience. Harris Wofford,* Bayard Rustin,* Glenn Smiley,* and Stanley Levison,* activists and associates of King, were very knowledgeable about the teachings of Gandhi, and helped instill in King the knowledge he needed to organize the social movement in Birmingham and the March on Washington* in 1963. In 1959, with the help of Wofford, King traveled to India to meet with Gandhi's family and Gandhian activists. On his return he stated, "Since being in India, I am more convinced than ever before that the method of nonviolent resistance is the most potent weapon available to oppressed people in their struggle for justice and human dignity."[1] When King received the Nobel Peace Prize in 1964, he praised Gandhi, saying, "He struggled only with the weapons of truth, soul force, non-injury, and courage."[2]

To combat racial discrimination, King and his followers recruited volunteers and delivered training workshops on nonviolence. However, public officials in Birmingham, Alabama, initially obstructed any protests with legal injunctions* (court orders backed by the police). These injunctions violated the freedom of association clauses of the First Amendment* to the Constitution of the United States* and, eventually, the movement exerted such pressure that it forced public officials to concede to the demands of the protestors.

Limitations

King made a crucial contribution to American democracy at a time when civil rights legislation was stalled in Congress.* He provided a detailed assessment of the history of racism in America, its current realities, and what could be done to overcome it in order to achieve reconciliation between white people and black people and thereby reach a higher level of humanity. This was done in the face of great defiance as many of Birmingham's city officials were deeply racist and, together with employers, sought to safeguard a system of oppression that was in many ways economically beneficial. His biggest rivals were George Wallace,* the governor of the state of Alabama, and Bull Connor,* the commissioner of public safety.

King's efforts in Birmingham and his March on Washington

shaped the passing of the Civil Rights Act of 1964* and the Voting Rights Act of 1965.* While African Americans have made much progress in many areas of society since then, King's dream of reconciliation, redemption, and equality have been limited by the persistence of racial discrimination in schooling, employment, policing, and the courts. While black people today remain disadvantaged when compared to white people in terms of social and economic opportunities, King's brave and vital contributions have served as an inspiration for activists worldwide.

NOTES

1   Cited in "Martin Luther King Recording Found in India," National Public Radio, January 16, 2009.

2   Martin Luther King Jr., "Nobel lecture," Oslo, Norway, December 11, 1964.

MODULE 8
PLACE IN THE AUTHOR'S WORK

KEY POINTS

- Through preaching, writing, and leading public demonstrations, Martin Luther King Jr. advanced the cause of African Americans from 1955 until his assassination in 1968.

- *Why We Can't Wait* was a crucial argument for combating racial discrimination and desegregating American society at a time when civil rights legislation was stalled in Congress.*

- King's work promoting civil disobedience* and nonviolent resistance has served as a source of inspiration for activists worldwide.

Positioning

Martin Luther King Jr.'s *Why We Can't Wait* was one of his many written contributions to the Civil Rights Movement* from 1955 until his assassination in 1968. King's philosophy was based on his father and grandfather's influence as Baptist ministers, his undergraduate and graduate training in theology and sociology, and the events he experienced. In 1955, just after finishing his PhD at Boston University, he became a Baptist minister himself and led the Montgomery Bus Boycott.* Two years later, he cofounded and became the first president of the Southern Christian Leadership Conference. Then, in 1959, he took a trip to India, where he met with the family of the political leader Mohandas Karmachand "Mahatma" Gandhi * and Gandhian activists, at which point he came to further understand and appreciate the value and techniques of nonviolent resistance. In 1962 and 1963, he led nonviolent protests against racism

> 66 Make a career of humanity. Commit yourself to the noble struggle for equal rights. You will make a greater person of yourself, a greater nation of your country, and a finer world to live in. 99
>
> Martin Luther King Jr., address at the Youth March for Integrated Schools on April 18, 1959

in Atlanta, Georgia, and Birmingham, Alabama. A year later, after delivering his "I Have a Dream"* speech following the March on Washington,* he was awarded the Nobel Peace Prize.

King engaged in activism through speeches, writings, sit-ins, boycotts, and marches. Prior to writing *Why We Can't Wait* (1964), King published three important works: *Stride Toward Freedom: The Montgomery Story* (1958), *The Measure of a Man* (1959), and *Strength to Love* (1963).

Integration

In *Stride Toward Freedom*, King describes the disturbing state of racism in Montgomery, Alabama, and explains the process and events that led up to the 1955 bus boycott, the nature of the event, and its aftermath. In one chapter, "Pilgrimage to Nonviolence," he explains how he shifted from seeing God as something merely metaphysical—in the sense of a purely spiritual force—to something that is part of his daily mindset and actions, and talks about how he came to adopt love and nonviolent protest as a way of life.

King went on to describe his conception of nonviolence: resistance to evil without the resort to physical contact, a means of searching for friendship and understanding in the enemy rather than an attempt to humiliate him or her. It was a matter of isolating the evil act rather than focusing on the person committing that evil. King made it clear that nonviolent protestors should endure suffering without retaliation because suffering is necessary for reconciliation and redemption. Finally, Christian morality and nonviolence require an unwavering faith in justice and humanity.

In *The Measure of a Man*, King explains in detail the relationship between Christianity and moral actions. Furthermore, he criticizes the gap between the founding values of the American republic—freedom, equality, and brotherhood—and the reality of three centuries of racism and inequality.

Strength to Love is a collection of King's sermons, which together transmit a passionate challenge to racial prejudice and the injustice that develops from it. He argues that we must always spread love against the evil force of hatred. In the text, he is also critical of those individuals who use the Bible as a pretext for demeaning others and committing violence. He shows how key figures in America did this during the period of slavery; the same was true during apartheid* in South Africa (a regime of legally enshrined racism).

Significance

From the age of 26 until his assassination at 39, King was a major influence in the United States and elsewhere. He delivered speeches, wrote books, preached in churches, and led nonviolent protests. His actions led to the passing of civil rights legislation, and made an important contribution to the subsequent progress of African Americans and other minorities. The fact that he became a martyr at such a young age has made him an iconic figure for activists.

King's life was a symbol of moral goodness, of doing what was right at all times, even if this led to imprisonment or death. His body of work links Christian morality to the wrongness of racial discrimination, and encourages individuals to oppose all laws that cause great human suffering; in this case, it was segregation.* He also encourages us to reflect on the link between economics, racism, and imperialism, to critique these, and to deal humanly with the suffering of others. King believes that we must strive to spread love at all times, refrain from any tendency toward violence, and seek to end injustice everywhere.

Throughout King's short life he voiced a prophetic sense of optimism that one day America would overcome its three centuries of injustice, and redeem its soul—that is, white and black people would live side by side in reconciliation and equality.

SECTION 3
IMPACT

MODULE 9
THE FIRST RESPONSES

KEY POINTS

- At the time of publication, some critics argued that African Americans had it much better than black people anywhere else, and that they were demanding too much. Others, such as the militant activist Malcolm X,* criticized the nonviolent approach, advocating instead separatism* and violent resistance.

- Many white, racist southerners, such as Alabama governor George Wallace,* argued that segregation* was best for white and black people and would ensure public order.

- Through his speeches, writings, and activism, King mobilized African Americans in large numbers in nonviolent protest and pressured public officials to pass civil rights legislation.

Criticism

While the author of *Why We Can't Wait*, Martin Luther King Jr., is widely understood today to be one of the great figures in American history and an influential figure globally, there was much less of a consensus in 1963. In fact, many politicians criticized him for his words and actions, claiming that African Americans should be content with what they had, rather than demanding more. The senator of South Carolina, Strom Thurmond,* stated, for example: "The Negroes in this country own more refrigerators, and more automobiles, than they do in any other country ... They are better fed, they are better clothed, they have better houses than in any other country in the world ... No one is deprived of freedom that I know about."[1] According to Senator Russell Long* of Indiana, meanwhile:

> **❝** Let us rise to the call for freedom-loving blood that is in us and send our answer to the tyranny that clanks its chains upon the South. In the name of the greatest people that have ever trod this earth, I draw the line in the dust and toss the gauntlet before the feet of tyranny, and I say segregation now, segregation tomorrow, segregation forever. **❞**
>
> George Wallace, inaugural speech of January 14, 1963

"Now what I as a Southerner plan to fight for is the right of a man to choose its neighbors among whom he will live, the right to decide who he is going to trade with, who's he going to do business with, who's he going to associate with."[2] Furthermore, a Gallup Poll taken in 1966 indicated that only 33 percent of Americans favored King's ideas.[3] In 1968, King was assassinated by James Earl Ray,* highlighting the extent to which racial hatred still existed despite the government's passing of civil rights legislation.

Responses

From 1955 until his assassination in 1968, King addressed all those who wished to prolong segregation in the United States; he did so with poise and humility, and by providing detailed, factual arguments that defended his campaign of nonviolent resistance. King firmly believed that racism and segregation were moral wrongs that had to be overcome, even if he lost his own life in the process. Perhaps his most memorable response to his critics at large came in 1963 at the Lincoln Memorial in Washington, DC, where he delivered his "I Have a Dream"* speech. In it, he stated: "I have a dream that one day down in Alabama, with its vicious racists, with its governor [George Wallace] having his lips dripping with the words 'interposition' and 'nullification'—one day right there in Alabama little black boys and black girls will be able to join hands with little white boys and white girls as sisters and brothers."[4] In 1965, King again responded to Governor Wallace's proud slogan "Segregation today, segregation tomorrow, segregation forever"[5] by stating:"Segregation is on its death bed in Alabama, and the only thing uncertain about it is how costly Wallace and the segregationists will make the funeral."[6]

Another important example of King calmly and persuasively responding to his critics was his "Letter from a Birmingham Jail," which he wrote on April 16, 1963 and which is included in *Why We Can't Wait*. In it, he defended his nonviolent resistance campaign against the criticisms of eight white clergymen who asked that King and his followers use the courts, rather than the streets, to demand civil rights. King disagreed with the common argument that the timing for the movement was not right by arguing that African Americans had already waited three hundred years for justice, and were still waiting.

Conflict and Consensus

During the Civil Rights Movement,* African American activists challenged racism and segregation through nonviolent resistance. This called into question the longstanding attitudes and practices of white America, and in particular white southerners. Some white people embraced progressive change and welcomed interracial contact, whereas others reacted with great hostility. The latter looked to racist public officials, such as Alabama's governor, George Wallace, who defended their views and way of life, denied racism, and claimed that black people had it good in America and were asking for too much.

The Civil Rights Movement exposed America's history of discrimination and exploitation, and the myths and dogmas that supported segregation. Black activists voiced their discontent through sit-ins, boycotts, marches, and protests, demanding dignity through nonviolent resistance on the streets. At the time, this was met with great opposition, and many would say the battle is not yet won, with some Americans still resisting white–black equality.

After King's March on Washington,* 77 percent of the American public viewed his actions unfavorably.[7] However, since his assassination in 1968 at the age of 39, many activists have glorified King's life, words, and actions, and looked to his speeches and writings for inspiration in their own struggles. The fact that there is now a federal holiday in the United States commemorating his contributions to American history highlights the extent to which there is some degree of consensus that he was one of the great figures in the country's history.

NOTES

1   Morgan Whitaker, "Back in the Day: What Critics Said about King's Speech in 1963," *MSNBC*, August 28, 2013.

2   Whitaker, "Back in the Day."

3   Whitaker, "Back in the Day."

4   Martin Luther King Jr., "I Have a Dream" speech, August 28, 1963.

5   George Wallace, "Inaugural address," Montgomery, Alabama, January 14, 1963.

6   Martin Luther King Jr., "Address at the conclusion of the Selma to Montgomery march," March 25, 1965.

7   Whitaker, "Back in the Day."

MODULE 10
THE EVOLVING DEBATE

KEY POINTS

- King and his followers waged a nonviolent struggle against racism, provoking white Americans to reflect on many issues; civil rights legislation followed, with the desegregation of public places and the granting of unimpeded voting rights to African Americans.

- King built on the ideas of Henry David Thoreau* and Mohandas Karmachand "Mahatma" Gandhi* in advocating a strategy of civil disobedience* and nonviolent resistance.

- The philosophers John Rawls* and Ronald Dworkin* have theorized further the concept of civil disobedience.

Uses And Problems

Martin Luther King Jr.'s *Why We Can't Wait*, published in 1964, was a summation of the author's long-standing civil rights struggle to that point. At a rally for the civil rights organization NAACP—the National Association for the Advancement of Colored People*—in 1957, King stated: "There is nothing greater in all the world than freedom. It's worth going to jail for. It's worth losing a job for. It's worth dying for. My friends, go out this evening determined to achieve this freedom which God wants for all of his children."[1]

Over the course of the past half-century, since King's assassination, his words and actions have served as an inspiration for those who have challenged unjust laws and struggled for greater freedom and equality.

During King's life, he was firmly committed to radically transforming American society through nonviolent activism, saying, "White America must recognize that justice for black people cannot be achieved without radical changes in the structure of our society."[2]

> **❝** Even today there still exists … the license that our society allows to unjust officials who implement their authority in the name of justice to practice injustice against minorities … If one doubts this conclusion, let him search the records and find how rarely … a police officer has been punished for abusing a Negro. **❞**
>
> Martin Luther King Jr., *Why We Can't Wait*

Through his speeches and writings, he aimed to highlight the moral wrongs of racism and inequality, and he encouraged an alternative, peaceful means of resolving conflict in an effort to achieve greater democracy. King was a prophet of justice who led the country out of the dark shadow of the Jim Crow* era and provided hope for a better tomorrow. The day before his death, he acknowledged, "We have some difficult days ahead. But it really doesn't matter with me now because I've been to the mountaintop … I've seen the Promised Land. I may not get there with you. But I want you to know tonight, that we, as a people, will get to the Promised Land."[3]

In this speech, King made it clear that racism and poverty were problems tied up with material interests and that overcoming them would require a long-term struggle. That struggle continues today.

Schools of Thought

King's philosophy of using civil disobedience to combat unjust laws that degrade humanity, and nonviolent resistance to counter racism and inequality, stems from the previous approaches of Thoreau and Gandhi. King emphasizes using the Christian doctrine of spreading love to confront hate, thereby encouraging oppressors to reflect on the evilness and injustice of their actions. For this reason, one of the chapters in the book that deals with nonviolence is called "The Sword that Heals."

King dedicated his adult life to fighting social evils and defending oppressed peoples everywhere. He increasingly understood the complex links between economics and racism and how economics shaped America's history of slavery and the segregationist* laws that defined the Jim Crow period.

He knew that due to three hundred years of discrimination toward black people, and the inequalities this had created, the nonviolent struggle would go well beyond his lifetime, and would be characterized by tensions, progress, and setbacks.

King's legacy as a civil rights leader has influenced a broad range of thinkers, from the minister and activist Jesse Jackson* to President Barack Obama,* as well as social movements around the world. Not all have agreed with King's nonviolent approach, however. Nelson Mandela,* for example, who waged a lifelong struggle against apartheid* in South Africa, shared King's commitment to freedom and equality, but considered violence an option when nonviolence failed in the face of extreme racism. Other radical figures and groups in history, such as Malcolm X,* Marcus Garvey,* and the militant organization known as the Black Panthers,* have shared King's commitment to combating racism and inequality, but, like Mandela, have adopted more violent approaches with the aim of achieving this.

In Current Scholarship

John Rawls is one scholar who has sought to further the concept of civil disobedience. In *Theory of Justice*, Rawls defines civil disobedience as a "public, nonviolent, conscientious yet political act contrary to law usually done with the aim of bringing about a change in the law or policies of the government."[4] He argues that it must "address the sense of justice of the majority of the community."[5] Thus, in contrast to King, he is unconcerned with the discrimination and inequalities faced by minority groups.

Ronald Dworkin is another scholar who has focused on civil

disobedience. He labels individual defiance of a law deemed immoral *justice-based disobedience*;* this he contrasts with *integrity-based disobedience*,* which occurs when an individual claims a right denied to him or her. He terms resistance to a law individuals consider wrong in order to change policy *policy-based civil disobedience*.*[6]

In addition to these theoretical, academic applications, King's philosophy has shaped a wide range of nonviolent demonstrations worldwide, ranging from the musician John Lennon* and the artist Yoko Ono's* protest against the Vietnam War* in 1969 to the protests in Eastern Europe at the end of the Cold War*—the tense, global nuclear standoff led by the United States and the Soviet Union.*

NOTES

1   Martin Luther King Jr., "Facing the challenge of a new age" address, delivered at NAACP Emancipation Day Rally, January 1, 1957.

2   Martin Luther King Jr., "A Testament of Hope," in *A Testament of Hope: The Essential Writings of Martin Luther King Jr.*, ed. James M. Washington (New York: Harper & Row, 1986), 194.

3   Martin Luther King Jr., "I've been to the mountaintop" sermon, Memphis, Tennessee, April 3, 1968.

4   John Rawls, *A Theory of Justice* (Cambridge, MA: Harvard University Press, 1971), 320.

5   Rawls, *Theory of Justice*, 364.

6   Ronald Dworkin, *A Matter of Principle* (Cambridge, MA: Harvard University Press, 1985).

MODULE 11
IMPACT AND INFLUENCE TODAY

KEY POINTS

- Martin Luther King Jr.'s philosophy, as detailed in *Why We Can't Wait*, continues to shape our modern-day understanding of civil disobedience* and to serve as an inspiration for social movements worldwide.

- King's active version of civil disobedience contrasts with the philosopher John Rawls's* theoretical, passive version; the former is concerned with injustice toward minorities, whereas the latter is concerned with the majority.

- Today, the focus of civil disobedience has become much broader, targeting a range of issues from environmental policy to criminal justice; in contrast to the 1960s, it now incorporates the Internet and social media.

Position

Martin Luther King Jr.'s *Why We Can't Wait* provides a poised, detailed, and persuasive account of racial discrimination in Birmingham, Alabama—both the most important industrial city and the most segregated in the South at the time. He wrote it in 1963, just a few months after the March on Washington,* where he delivered his famous "I Have a Dream"* speech; as the title suggests, it aims to document the state of discrimination toward African Americans and what needs to be done to address it. In doing so, King focuses his attention on Bull Connor,* a powerful city commissioner in Birmingham, who sought to terrorize black people through the use of policing and courts. King then highlights the bravery of ordinary citizens, whose deep faith made them push forward against all odds in their determined pursuit of justice. His "Letter from Birmingham Jail"

> ❝ In the face of hatred, they prayed for their tormentors. In the face of violence, they stood up and sat in with the moral force of nonviolence. Willingly, they went to jail to protest unjust laws, their cells swelling with the sound of freedom songs. A lifetime of indignities had taught them that no man could take away the dignity and grace that God grants us. They had learned through hard experience what Frederick Douglass once taught: that freedom is not given; it must be won through struggle and discipline, persistence and faith. ❞
>
> President Barack Obama's speech on the 50th anniversary of the March on Washington

(1963), included as one of the eight chapters of *Why We Can't Wait*, is an eloquent response to his critics (eight white clergymen), and details why the nonviolent resistance movement is a necessary response to racism.

King targets his message at both blatant white racists and more discreet white moderates. He criticizes the former for trying to safeguard segregation,* while he chastises the latter for promoting order over justice. He makes it clear that these individuals should be seen as the perpetrators of chaos, and not the protestors, who are simply demonstrating for equal rights.

The text is a very important account of the Civil Rights Movement,* and King's nonviolent approach has served as an inspiration for social movements for over half a century.

Interaction

King and the American philosopher John Rawls, a thinker concerned with questions of ethics, have very different conceptions of civil disobedience. Rawls believes that citizens are part of a social contract*—that is, they have agreed to give up some freedom for the collective welfare and security of all; this discourages acts of resistance that challenge the majority norm and disrupt public order, even in cases in which minorities consider laws to be unjust. In his *A Theory of Justice* (1971), Rawls argues that civil disobedience is permissible only when injustice threatens the majority of society. Writing from the position of a privileged, white academic, his argument is philosophical and purely theoretical. That is to say, he does not apply it to a particular case, such as racial discrimination toward African Americans or gender discrimination toward women, but rather he considers civil disobedience as an abstract and hypothetical situation.

On the other hand, King was a Baptist minister, whose life was threatened, and who sought to achieve tangible results for black people suffering as a result of racial discrimination and segregation. He applies the concept of civil disobedience to deprived minorities, and seeks to challenge the unjust laws that shaped their oppression. King's man-of-action vision also contrasts with many white, Christian ministers who, like Rawls, adopted a passive attitude, arguing that black people should use the court system rather than utilizing nonviolent protest on the streets.

Rawls's passive notion of civil disobedience, then, must be seen as very different from King's active notion based on the ideas of Henry David Thoreau* and Mohandas Karmachand Gandhi.*

The Continuing Debate

At the time King published *Why We Can't Wait*, his main emphasis was on the use of nonviolence to pressure the American government to desegregate public institutions and grant black people the unconditional right to vote. Since the Civil Rights Movement, there has been a shift in the goals of civil disobedience. King's approach was consistent with the previous approaches used by Gandhi and the Suffragettes* (female campaigners for the right to vote), for example.

In recent years, social movements have encompassed a much broader focus, seeking reforms in areas ranging from environmental policy to criminal justice to minimum wage laws, and have depended heavily on the Internet and social media. For example, Black Lives Matter,* a predominantly nonviolent social movement, has responded to a wave of racist police shootings in the United States that have been captured on film by calling for greater police accountability. The movement has organized mixed sit-ins, boycotts, and demonstrations with a prolific use of social media in order to create greater public consciousness and pressure for reform.

The fact that we see such social movements today is a testament to the enduring phenomenon of racial discrimination, which shapes inequality in such areas as education, the workplace, and criminal justice. The strategy of Black Lives Matter is similar to King's insofar as it seeks to hold blatant, white racists accountable, and also pressures white moderates, who may acknowledge that racism is a problem but do not act against it.

MODULE 12
WHERE NEXT?

KEY POINTS

- *Why We Can't Wait* was an important contribution to the Civil Rights Movement.* It explained the process and events leading up to the "Negro Revolution"* of 1963, and pressured government to pass civil rights legislation.

- Since the book's publication, it has served as an important account of the period 1955–63, and has inspired nonviolent struggles for greater freedom and equality.

- As racial discrimination and inequality are still major problems in education, employment, and criminal justice, among other areas, King's philosophy and vision are still highly relevant today, though the scope of resistance has become broader and now incorporates Internet technology and social media.

Potential

Martin Luther King's *Why We Can't Wait* will likely continue to serve as an important historical account of the Civil Rights Movement from 1955 through 1963. King was the most prominent black leader in the United States at the time of publication, and remains one of the key figures in American history. Furthermore, King's vision of social justice, and his nonviolent approach to achieving it, will likely continue to inspire activists globally. For many, he is an iconic figure because of his commitment to freedom and equality, and because he died a martyr at such a young age.

King's activism and body of scholarly work address a number of key themes that remain of great relevance today. These include racial discrimination, urban segregation,* unequal opportunities in education

> **"** We have more to do to bring Dr. King's dream within reach of all our daughters and sons. We must stand together for good jobs, fair wages, safe neighborhoods, and quality education. With one voice, we must ensure the scales of justice work equally for all—considering not only how justice is applied, but also how it is perceived and experienced. As Dr. King told us, 'injustice anywhere is a threat to justice everywhere,' and this remains our great unfinished business. **"**
>
> Barack Obama, presidential proclamation commemorating the Martin Luther King Jr. federal holiday

and employment, poverty, imprisonment, and police violence.

Today, these issues continue to resound. For example, unemployment among black people is 2–2.5 times higher than for white people,[1] and the incarceration rate for black people is six times higher than for white people.[2]

If King were alive today, he would likely be consoled by the fact that America has now had its first black president, Barack Obama—a sign of considerable progress. But it is probable he would also be deeply concerned by the enduring problems that plague American society. In combating inequalities, his attention would likely be focused on raising the minimum wage, protecting, or perhaps expanding, social security and state-funded medical programs such as "Medicare,"* struggling against racial discrimination, tackling mass incarceration, holding the police accountable for violence toward black youths such as Freddie Gray* (a black resident of Baltimore, Maryland, who died from a spinal cord injury at the hands of police in April 2015), raising taxes on the rich, and redistributing wealth to benefit the working and middle classes.

Future Directions

Events such as the Baltimore riots* of 2015, sparked by the death of Freddie Gray, and social movements like Black Lives Matter* highlight the extent to which racial discrimination and inequality continue to be major problems in American society. The protests in Baltimore came in response to a series of police shootings of unarmed black men, and highlighted deeper problems, including urban segregation and economic inequality.

Although the Civil Rights Movement of the 1950s and 1960s shaped the emergence of a black middle class, and greater black political participation—as highlighted by, for example, Barack Obama,* and Eric Holder,* the first ever African American attorney general—working-class black people continue to be plagued by a variety of problems, including disproportionate unemployment, poverty, and incarceration.

The Obama administration has carried out a number of positive initiatives in response to these killings and the emergence of Black Lives Matters, including pushing to reduce prison populations, granting mass clemency to nonviolent drug offenders, and carrying out federal investigations into policing abuses. All of these endeavors are loyal to the ideas of Martin Luther King Jr., who sought to address the evils of systemic racism.

Despite these positive initiatives, however, the Obama administration has, to date, prosecuted few police officers for their misconduct. If King were alive today, he would probably be deeply concerned by this, and would push for a more genuine commitment to racial justice. One such case is that of Darren Wilson,* whom the courts acquitted after he killed the unarmed African American Michael Brown* in Ferguson, Missouri, in 2014. King would likely also criticize black figures in public office for not doing more to combat these problems.

Issues such as racial profiling, mass incarceration, police violence, and unequal education and employment opportunities will likely continue to attract much attention in the future. While society has progressed in many ways since Martin Luther King Jr., as highlighted by the number of black figures in high political offices, great challenges clearly remain.

Summary

In *Why We Can't Wait*, Martin Luther King Jr. describes in detail the process and events leading up to the "Negro Revolution" of 1963. The text covers the history of black oppression in the United States as well as racism and segregation at the time, and articulates a mounting frustration among African Americans. In 1954, the Supreme Court* case *Brown vs. the Board of Education** called for desegregation in public schools. By 1963, however, only a small number of Southern schools had desegregated. Despite progressive campaign promises, both the Democrats* and the Republicans* turned a blind eye to this reality. Black people in the United States became frustrated with this injustice, and sought to follow the trend of anticolonial struggles in Africa and Asia by fighting for greater liberty. It was logical for this to occur in 1963, as it marked the 100-year anniversary of President Abraham Lincoln's* Emancipation Proclamation,* which formally outlawed slavery.

King details how he and other civil rights leaders trained volunteers to protest in Birmingham, and how their brave efforts led to a promise from authorities to desegregate city schools, open up jobs to black people, release prisoners jailed during demonstrations, and engage in further dialogue about racism. This was a major accomplishment considering that Birmingham was both the most important industrial city in the South and the most segregated urban location in the country.

Finally, King reflects on the difficult days ahead, and argues that, for black people to close the gap of three centuries of injustice, they would have to unite closer with other oppressed groups, including deprived members of the white working class. This would be necessary to make authorities listen and carry out radical reforms.

NOTES

1   Neil Irwin et al., "America's Racial Divide Chartered," *The New York Times*, August 19, 2014.

2   George Gao, "Chart of the Week: The Black–White Gap in Incarceration Rates," Pew Research Center, July 18, 2014.

GLOSSARY

GLOSSARY OF TERMS

Abolitionists: those who fought to end slavery in the United States and elsewhere.

Alabama Christian Movement for Human Rights: a civil rights organization formed in Birmingham, Alabama, by Reverend Fred Shuttlesworth that organized sit-ins, boycotts, and other forms of protest during the 1950s and 1960s.

American Civil War (1861–65): a war fought in the United States between Northern (Union) and Southern (Confederate) states. The immediate cause of the conflict was over the expansion of slavery in the US and over cotton and other trading between the states.

Apartheid: a system of racial discrimination and segregation in the Republic of South Africa from 1948 to 1994.

Baltimore riots: a series of protests that took place in Baltimore, Maryland, in April 2015 in response to police violence toward African Americans. The injury and later death of Freddie Gray at the hands of police sparked the uprising.

Baptist: a member of the Protestant Church who believes in freedom of consciousness, the separation of Church and State, and in baptizing believers who are conscious of the act of baptism.

Bible: the holy book of Christianity.

Black Lives Matter: an activist movement formed in 2013 in response to police shootings of African Americans; it campaigns for police accountability and reform of the criminal justice system.

Black Panthers: a black militant political organization active between 1966 and 1982.

Brown vs. the Board of Education: a landmark Supreme Court case in 1954 that overturned *Plessy vs. Ferguson* (1896) by ruling racial segregation in the public schools of the United States to be unconstitutional.

Capitalism: an economic system founded on the private ownership of trade and the means of production (those things, such as land, natural resources, and technology, that are necessary for the production of goods).

Christian morals: the teaching of right and wrong behavior derived from biblical scripture (and, to a lesser extent, in secular communities originally founded on Christian moral principles).

Civil disobedience: the action of disobeying unjust laws; the principle that this is morally permissible and even necessary.

Civil Rights Act (1964): an act signed into law by President Lyndon Johnson banning racial discrimination in public places, and declaring discrimination in employment illegal.

Civil Rights Movement: several organized strands of political and social action in the 1950s and 1960s, in which black citizens of the United States and their allies struggled against discrimination and for greater equality.

Cold War: a period of tension from 1947–91 between the United States and its Western allies and the Eastern federation of countries known as the Soviet Union.

Communism: a political ideology founded on state ownership of the means of production, the collectivization of labor, and the abolition of social class.

Congress: in the US, the legislative body of the federal government. It consists of two houses: the lower chamber (the House of Representatives) and the upper chamber (the Senate).

Constitution of the United States: a document adopted in 1787 and ratified in 1788 that acts as the supreme law of the United States of America. It outlines the civil rights and liberties afforded to citizens, considers unconstitutional any attempts by the states to nullify its laws, and details a system of checks and balances between the three main branches of government: the executive, the legislative, and the judicial.

The Crisis: the official magazine of the National Association for the Advancement of Colored People (NAACP); it was founded in 1910 by W. E. B. Du Bois.

Declaration of Independence: the declaration, made on 4 July, 1776 by 13 of Britain's North American colonies, that they considered themselves independent of the British crown. The event marked the founding of the United States of America.

Democratic Party: an American political party that initially developed in the 1790s from antifederalist factions that favored states' rights.

Disenfranchised: an adjective used to describe those who lose certain rights, in particular the right to vote.

Emancipation Proclamation: an act issued by President Abraham Lincoln in 1863, in the midst of the American Civil War. It established that all persons held as slaves in the rebellious Southern states would henceforth be free.

First Amendment: an amendment to the Constitution of the United States adopted in 1791 that established freedom of speech, assembly, press, and religion.

"I Have a Dream" speech: a landmark speech delivered by Martin Luther King Jr. at the Lincoln Memorial in Washington, DC on August 28, 1963. There were over 250,000 people present, and it called for equality for African Americans.

Injunction: a court order used to stop a public protest. This was a common tactic used by public officials to break up demonstrations during the Civil Rights Movement.

Integrity-based disobedience: challenge by an individual or group to a law they deem immoral and degrading.

Iraq War (2003–11): a conflict that began in 2003 when a coalition, led by the United States and Britain, invaded Iraq with the aim of overthrowing the existing regime led by Saddam Hussein's Baathist Party, which was achieved that same year.

Jim Crow: a period in American history from the end of Reconstruction until the Civil Rights Movement of the 1950s and 1960s when the state and federal governments put a number of impediments in place to prevent black people from reaching greater equality. This included segregation of public spaces, obstacles to voting, and unequal economic opportunities.

Justice-based disobedience: challenge to a law by an individual or group because they have been denied a right.

Literacy tests: tests administered at the discretion of voting officials during the period known as Jim Crow. They impeded the right to vote of African Americans, and sometimes poor white people.

March on Washington: a march led by Martin Luther King Jr. in Washington, DC. On August 28, 1963, over 200,000 people assembled at the Lincoln Memorial to listen to King deliver his "I Have a Dream" speech.

Medicare: the US government's health insurance for people 65 years of age and over.

Mexican–American War: an armed conflict between Mexico and the United States (1846–48), which provoked tensions between the South and the North over whether the acquired territories would be free or slave states.

Montgomery Bus Boycott: one of the key moments in the Civil Rights Movement, which took place in 1955; it refers to the refusal of African Americans to give up their seats in white-only designated areas.

National Association for the Advancement of Colored People (NAACP): a black civil rights organization formed by W. E. B. Du Bois and other activists in 1909. It struggled to end racism and achieve equality.

"Negro Revolution": a term coined by Martin Luther King Jr. to refer to the mass, nonviolent uprising of African Americans against racial discrimination in 1963.

Peaceable Kingdom: a place documented in the Bible, in which lions and lambs coexisted in absolutely perfect harmony.

Policy-based civil disobedience: challenge to a law, by an individual or group, because they deem it unjust, with the objective of changing policy.

Poll Tax: a tax required in order to vote.

Reconstruction: the period from 1865–77 when the federal government of the United States reincorporated the Southern states into the union and rebuilt political and social structures compromised in the years of the American Civil War.

Republicans (Republican Party): a political party founded in 1854, mainly composed of antislavery activists.

Satyagraha: ("life-force") a philosophy developed by Mohandas Karmachand "Mahatma" Gandhi, which advocated confronting hatred with nonviolent protest in order to achieve political, economic, and social reforms.

Segregation: the separation of people of different races or class.

Separatism: the belief that different groups, for instance, black and white people, should form their own distinct nations.

Social contract: a voluntary agreement made by an individual to give up perfect liberty so that collective welfare and security might be better secured.

Social mobility: the movement of individuals, families, or groups from one social class or status to another.

Suffragettes: women who pursued the right to vote. Their struggles in America led to the eventual ratification of the Nineteenth Amendment to the Constitution of the United States, which granted women suffrage.

Supreme Court: a federal court in the United States that acts as the supreme interpreter of the constitution and holds ultimate power over all federal and state courts. It considers unconstitutional any attempt by states to nullify its laws.

Talented Tenth: a term used by W. E. B. Du Bois in his book *The Souls of Black Folk* (1903); he argued that African Americans need a leadership class or Talented Tenth to advance equality in America.

USSR: the Union of Soviet Socialist Republics, a federal union of 15 socialist republics that existed in Eastern Europe and Northern Asia from 1922 to 1991.

Utopia: an ideally perfect place.

Vietnam War: a military conflict lasting from 1955 to 1975 between South Vietnam, supported by the United States, and communist North Vietnam. Between 1965 and 1972, the United States fought in the war on behalf of South Vietnam.

Voting Rights Act (1965): an act that ruled unconstitutional all conditions (such as literacy tests and poll taxes) that impede the right of individuals to vote in the United States.

PEOPLE MENTIONED IN THE TEXT

Michael Brown (1996–2014) was an African American youth shot and killed by police in Ferguson, Missouri, on August 9, 2014.

Jesus Christ (c. 4 B.C.E.– C.E. 29) was a teacher and prophet, whose life and sermons form the basis of Christianity.

Theophilus Eugene "Bull" Connor (1897–1973), remembered as a symbol of American institutional racism, was commissioner of public safety for the city of Birmingham, Alabama, during King's leadership of the civil rights action there. He sought to enforce racial segregation and deny rights to the city's black citizens.

Frederick Douglass (1818–95) was an escaped slave who became a prominent abolitionist, author, and public speaker.
W. E. B. Du Bois (1868–1963) was a prominent teacher, researcher, journalist, and activist. He was the first African American to graduate from Harvard University, and is the author of *The Souls of Black Folk* (1903), among many other important works.

Ronald Dworkin (1931–2013) was an American philosopher best known for his "interpretivist" approach to law, which stresses the importance of paying attention both to the facts and the values behind legal practices.

Mohandas Karmachand Gandhi (1869–1948) was the leader of a peaceful Indian independence movement against British rule. He advocated civil disobedience against injustice.

Marcus Garvey (1887–1940) was a Jamaican activist who advocated black separatism. He founded the Black Star Line, which promoted the return of all black people to Africa—even those born in the United States.

Freddie Gray (1989–2015) was a black resident of Baltimore, Maryland, who died from a spinal cord injury at the hands of police in April 2015.

Eric Holder (b. 1951), was an American judge and lawyer, and the first African American to hold the position of US attorney general.

Jesse Jackson (b. 1941) is a black Baptist minister and politician, prominent in the struggle for advancing equality in America.

Lyndon Baines Johnson (1908–73) was the 36th president of the United States. He was notable for his efforts to bring about the passage of the Civil Rights Act and Voting Rights Act.

John F. Kennedy (1917–63) was the 35th president of the United States. He was assassinated in November 1963.

John Lennon (1940–80) was a musician; he was a member of the deeply influential band the Beatles and a pacifist.

Stanley Levison (1912–79) was a Jewish businessmen and a social activist.
Abraham Lincoln (1809–65) was the 16th president of the United States. He issued the Emancipation Proclamation in 1863.

Russell Long (1918–2003) was senator from Louisiana from 1948 to 1987.

Martin Luther (1483–1546) was a German philosopher and religious figure who initiated the Protestant Reformation, which was a major movement in sixteenth-century Europe that reformed the beliefs and practices of the Catholic Church.

Nelson Mandela (1918–2013) was president of South Africa from 1994 to 1999. He was a figurehead of the struggle against South African apartheid, for which he spent nearly 30 years in jail.

Karl Marx (1818–83) was a German philosopher and economist, and a significant figure in the International Workingmen's Association. His philosophy, Marxism, remains foundational in many disciplines.

Barack Obama (b. 1961) is the 44th president of the United States. He assumed office in 2009.

Yoko Ono (b. 1933) is a peace activist and artist who was also was the second wife of John Lennon.

Rosa Parks (1913–2005) was a civil rights activist, and is known for refusing to give up her seat at the Montgomery Bus Boycott.

John Rawls (1921–2002) was an American philosopher, best known for *A Theory of Justice* (1971).

James Earl Ray (1928–98) was convicted of assassinating Martin Luther King Jr. and sentenced to life imprisonment.

Josiah Royce (1855–1916) was a philosopher who wrote *The Problem of Christianity* (1913). In it, he spoke of a "beloved community," grounded in the idea that an entire community accepts the hardships of history, and intuitively feels that words and actions which affect certain members of that community affect everyone.

Bayard Rustin (1912–87) was an American activist who worked with Gandhian activists in India, and then alongside Martin Luther King Jr. in the United States, promoting civil disobedience and nonviolent resistance. He was an important figure in the planning and implementation of the 1963 March on Washington.

Coretta Scott (1927–2006) was a civil rights activist and the wife of Martin Luther King Jr. from 1953–68.

Fred Shuttlesworth (1922–2011) was a Baptist minister and a civil rights activist in Alabama.

Glenn Smiley (1910–93) was a preacher and civil rights activist, and a close associate of Martin Luther King Jr.

Henry David Thoreau (1817–62) was an American author best known for the works *Civil Disobedience* (1849) and *Walden* (1854). He argued that it was the moral and civil duty of all citizens to oppose unjust laws.

Strom Thurmond (1902–2003) was senator of South Carolina for 48 years, and a major opponent of civil rights legislation.

Wyatt Walker (b. 1929) is an African American minister and civil rights leader who secretly traveled throughout Birmingham, Alabama, in order to establish the logistics of civil rights demonstrations.

George Wallace (1919–98) was an American politician who was the 45th governor of Alabama; he is remembered as an advocate of segregation.

Booker T. Washington (1856–1915) was a civil rights activist and the most important African American leader from around 1890 to 1915. He advocated accommodating white racism in exchange for rights.

Darren Wilson (b. 1986) was the police officer who shot and killed 18-year-old African American youth Michael Brown in Ferguson, Missouri, on August 9, 2014.

Harris Wofford (b. 1926) is a lawyer, civil rights activist, member of the Democratic Party, and a former senator of Pennsylvania.

Malcolm X (1925–65) was a black activist who advocated black supremacy, separatism, and militancy. His philosophy differed greatly from Martin Luther King Jr.'s doctrine of nonviolent resistance.

WORKS CITED

WORKS CITED

Carson, Clayborne, ed. *The Papers of Martin Luther King Jr.* Vol. V. Berkeley and Los Angeles: University of California Press, 2005.

Dworkin, Ronald. *A Matter of Principle*. Cambridge, MA: Harvard University Press, 1985.

Gandhi, Mahatma. "Speech." December 20, 1926. In Gandhi, *Gandhi: All Men Are Brothers*. Edited by Krishna Kripalani. New York: Continuum International Publishing Group, 2011.

————. "Speech on non-violence." September 11, 1906.

Gao, George. "Chart of the Week: The Black-White Gap in Incarceration Rates." Pew Research Center, July 18, 2014.

King, Martin Luther, Jr. "Address at the conclusion of the Selma to Montgomery march." March 25, 1965.

————. "The birth of a new nation" sermon. Montgomery, Alabama, April 7, 1957.

————. "Facing the challenge of a new age" address. Delivered at NAACP Emancipation Day Rally, January 1, 1957.

————. "I Have a Dream" speech. August 28, 1963.

————. "I've been to the mountaintop" sermon. Memphis, Tennessee, April 3, 1968.

————. "Nobel lecture." Oslo, Norway, December 11, 1964.

————. *Strength to Love*. Minneapolis: Fortress Press, 2010.

————. "A Testament of Hope." In *A Testament of Hope: The Essential Writings of Martin Luther King Jr.* Edited by James M. Washington, 313–1. New York: Harper & Row, 1986.

————. "Where do we go from here?" speech. Southern Christian Leadership Conference, Atlanta, Georgia, August 16, 1967.

————. "Why I am opposed to the war in Vietnam" sermon. Riverside Church, New York, April, 30, 1967.

————. *Why We Can't Wait*. New York: Penguin, 2000.

"Martin Luther King Recording Found in India." National Public Radio, January 16, 2009.

Irwin, Neil, Claire Cain Miller, and Margot Sanger Katz. "America's Racial Divide Chartered." *The New York Times*, August 19, 2014.

Rawls, John. *A Theory of Justice*. Cambridge, MA: Harvard University Press, 1971.

Wallace, George. "Inaugural address." Montgomery, Alabama, January 14, 1963.

Whitaker, Morgan. "Back in the Day: What Critics Said about King's Speech in 1963." *MSNBC*, August 28, 2013.

THE MACAT LIBRARY
BY DISCIPLINE

AFRICANA STUDIES

Chinua Achebe's *An Image of Africa: Racism in Conrad's Heart of Darkness*
W. E. B. Du Bois's *The Souls of Black Folk*
Zora Neale Huston's *Characteristics of Negro Expression*
Martin Luther King Jr's *Why We Can't Wait*
Toni Morrison's *Playing in the Dark: Whiteness in the American Literary Imagination*

ANTHROPOLOGY

Arjun Appadurai's *Modernity at Large: Cultural Dimensions of Globalisation*
Philippe Ariès's *Centuries of Childhood*
Franz Boas's *Race, Language and Culture*
Kim Chan & Renée Mauborgne's *Blue Ocean Strategy*
Jared Diamond's *Guns, Germs & Steel: the Fate of Human Societies*
Jared Diamond's *Collapse: How Societies Choose to Fail or Survive*
E. E. Evans-Pritchard's *Witchcraft, Oracles and Magic Among the Azande*
James Ferguson's *The Anti-Politics Machine*
Clifford Geertz's *The Interpretation of Cultures*
David Graeber's *Debt: the First 5000 Years*
Karen Ho's *Liquidated: An Ethnography of Wall Street*
Geert Hofstede's *Culture's Consequences: Comparing Values, Behaviors, Institutes and Organizations across Nations*
Claude Lévi-Strauss's *Structural Anthropology*
Jay Macleod's *Ain't No Makin' It: Aspirations and Attainment in a Low-Income Neighborhood*
Saba Mahmood's *The Politics of Piety: The Islamic Revival and the Feminist Subjec*t
Marcel Mauss's *The Gift*

BUSINESS

Jean Lave & Etienne Wenger's *Situated Learning*
Theodore Levitt's *Marketing Myopia*
Burton G. Malkiel's *A Random Walk Down Wall Street*
Douglas McGregor's *The Human Side of Enterprise*
Michael Porter's *Competitive Strategy: Creating and Sustaining Superior Performance*
John Kotter's *Leading Change*
C. K. Prahalad & Gary Hamel's *The Core Competence of the Corporation*

CRIMINOLOGY

Michelle Alexander's *The New Jim Crow: Mass Incarceration in the Age of Colorblindness*
Michael R. Gottfredson & Travis Hirschi's *A General Theory of Crime*
Richard Herrnstein & Charles A. Murray's *The Bell Curve: Intelligence and Class Structure in American Life*
Elizabeth Loftus's *Eyewitness Testimony*
Jay Macleod's *Ain't No Makin' It: Aspirations and Attainment in a Low-Income Neighborhood*
Philip Zimbardo's *The Lucifer Effect*

ECONOMICS

Janet Abu-Lughod's *Before European Hegemony*
Ha-Joon Chang's *Kicking Away the Ladder*
David Brion Davis's *The Problem of Slavery in the Age of Revolution*
Milton Friedman's *The Role of Monetary Policy*
Milton Friedman's *Capitalism and Freedom*
David Graeber's *Debt: the First 5000 Years*
Friedrich Hayek's *The Road to Serfdom*
Karen Ho's *Liquidated: An Ethnography of Wall Street*

John Maynard Keynes's *The General Theory of Employment, Interest and Money*
Charles P. Kindleberger's *Manias, Panics and Crashes*
Robert Lucas's *Why Doesn't Capital Flow from Rich to Poor Countries?*
Burton G. Malkiel's *A Random Walk Down Wall Street*
Thomas Robert Malthus's *An Essay on the Principle of Population*
Karl Marx's *Capital*
Thomas Piketty's *Capital in the Twenty-First Century*
Amartya Sen's *Development as Freedom*
Adam Smith's *The Wealth of Nations*
Nassim Nicholas Taleb's *The Black Swan: The Impact of the Highly Improbable*
Amos Tversky's & Daniel Kahneman's *Judgment under Uncertainty: Heuristics and Biases*
Mahbub Ul Haq's *Reflections on Human Development*
Max Weber's *The Protestant Ethic and the Spirit of Capitalism*

FEMINISM AND GENDER STUDIES

Judith Butler's *Gender Trouble*
Simone De Beauvoir's *The Second Sex*
Michel Foucault's *History of Sexuality*
Betty Friedan's *The Feminine Mystique*
Saba Mahmood's *The Politics of Piety: The Islamic Revival and the Feminist Subject*
Joan Wallach Scott's *Gender and the Politics of History*
Mary Wollstonecraft's *A Vindication of the Rights of Woman*
Virginia Woolf's *A Room of One's Own*

GEOGRAPHY

The Brundtland Report's *Our Common Future*
Rachel Carson's *Silent Spring*
Charles Darwin's *On the Origin of Species*
James Ferguson's *The Anti-Politics Machine*
Jane Jacobs's *The Death and Life of Great American Cities*
James Lovelock's *Gaia: A New Look at Life on Earth*
Amartya Sen's *Development as Freedom*
Mathis Wackernagel & William Rees's *Our Ecological Footprint*

HISTORY

Janet Abu-Lughod's *Before European Hegemony*
Benedict Anderson's *Imagined Communities*
Bernard Bailyn's *The Ideological Origins of the American Revolution*
Hanna Batatu's *The Old Social Classes And The Revolutionary Movements Of Iraq*
Christopher Browning's *Ordinary Men: Reserve Police Batallion 101 and the Final Solution in Poland*
Edmund Burke's *Reflections on the Revolution in France*
William Cronon's *Nature's Metropolis: Chicago And The Great West*
Alfred W. Crosby's *The Columbian Exchange*
Hamid Dabashi's *Iran: A People Interrupted*
David Brion Davis's *The Problem of Slavery in the Age of Revolution*
Nathalie Zemon Davis's *The Return of Martin Guerre*
Jared Diamond's *Guns, Germs & Steel: the Fate of Human Societies*
Frank Dikotter's *Mao's Great Famine*
John W Dower's *War Without Mercy: Race And Power In The Pacific War*
W. E. B. Du Bois's *The Souls of Black Folk*
Richard J. Evans's *In Defence of History*
Lucien Febvre's *The Problem of Unbelief in the 16th Century*
Sheila Fitzpatrick's *Everyday Stalinism*

Eric Foner's *Reconstruction: America's Unfinished Revolution, 1863-1877*
Michel Foucault's *Discipline and Punish*
Michel Foucault's *History of Sexuality*
Francis Fukuyama's *The End of History and the Last Man*
John Lewis Gaddis's *We Now Know: Rethinking Cold War History*
Ernest Gellner's *Nations and Nationalism*
Eugene Genovese's *Roll, Jordan, Roll: The World the Slaves Made*
Carlo Ginzburg's *The Night Battles*
Daniel Goldhagen's *Hitler's Willing Executioners*
Jack Goldstone's *Revolution and Rebellion in the Early Modern World*
Antonio Gramsci's *The Prison Notebooks*
Alexander Hamilton, John Jay & James Madison's *The Federalist Papers*
Christopher Hill's *The World Turned Upside Down*
Carole Hillenbrand's *The Crusades: Islamic Perspectives*
Thomas Hobbes's *Leviathan*
Eric Hobsbawm's *The Age Of Revolution*
John A. Hobson's *Imperialism: A Study*
Albert Hourani's *History of the Arab Peoples*
Samuel P. Huntington's *The Clash of Civilizations and the Remaking of World Order*
C. L. R. James's *The Black Jacobins*
Tony Judt's *Postwar: A History of Europe Since 1945*
Ernst Kantorowicz's *The King's Two Bodies: A Study in Medieval Political Theology*
Paul Kennedy's *The Rise and Fall of the Great Powers*
Ian Kershaw's *The "Hitler Myth": Image and Reality in the Third Reich*
John Maynard Keynes's *The General Theory of Employment, Interest and Money*
Charles P. Kindleberger's *Manias, Panics and Crashes*
Martin Luther King Jr's *Why We Can't Wait*
Henry Kissinger's *World Order: Reflections on the Character of Nations and the Course of History*
Thomas Kuhn's *The Structure of Scientific Revolutions*
Georges Lefebvre's *The Coming of the French Revolution*
John Locke's *Two Treatises of Government*
Niccolò Machiavelli's *The Prince*
Thomas Robert Malthus's *An Essay on the Principle of Population*
Mahmood Mamdani's *Citizen and Subject: Contemporary Africa And The Legacy Of Late Colonialism*
Karl Marx's *Capital*
Stanley Milgram's *Obedience to Authority*
John Stuart Mill's *On Liberty*
Thomas Paine's *Common Sense*
Thomas Paine's *Rights of Man*
Geoffrey Parker's *Global Crisis: War, Climate Change and Catastrophe in the Seventeenth Century*
Jonathan Riley-Smith's *The First Crusade and the Idea of Crusading*
Jean-Jacques Rousseau's *The Social Contract*
Joan Wallach Scott's *Gender and the Politics of History*
Theda Skocpol's *States and Social Revolutions*
Adam Smith's *The Wealth of Nations*
Timothy Snyder's *Bloodlands: Europe Between Hitler and Stalin*
Sun Tzu's *The Art of War*
Keith Thomas's *Religion and the Decline of Magic*
Thucydides's *The History of the Peloponnesian War*
Frederick Jackson Turner's *The Significance of the Frontier in American History*
Odd Arne Westad's *The Global Cold War: Third World Interventions And The Making Of Our Times*

LITERATURE

Chinua Achebe's *An Image of Africa: Racism in Conrad's Heart of Darkness*
Roland Barthes's *Mythologies*
Homi K. Bhabha's *The Location of Culture*
Judith Butler's *Gender Trouble*
Simone De Beauvoir's *The Second Sex*
Ferdinand De Saussure's *Course in General Linguistics*
T. S. Eliot's *The Sacred Wood: Essays on Poetry and Criticism*
Zora Neale Huston's *Characteristics of Negro Expression*
Toni Morrison's *Playing in the Dark: Whiteness in the American Literary Imagination*
Edward Said's *Orientalism*
Gayatri Chakravorty Spivak's *Can the Subaltern Speak?*
Mary Wollstonecraft's *A Vindication of the Rights of Women*
Virginia Woolf's *A Room of One's Own*

PHILOSOPHY

Elizabeth Anscombe's *Modern Moral Philosophy*
Hannah Arendt's *The Human Condition*
Aristotle's *Metaphysics*
Aristotle's *Nicomachean Ethics*
Edmund Gettier's *Is Justified True Belief Knowledge?*
Georg Wilhelm Friedrich Hegel's *Phenomenology of Spirit*
David Hume's *Dialogues Concerning Natural Religion*
David Hume's *The Enquiry for Human Understanding*
Immanuel Kant's *Religion within the Boundaries of Mere Reason*
Immanuel Kant's *Critique of Pure Reason*
Søren Kierkegaard's *The Sickness Unto Death*
Søren Kierkegaard's *Fear and Trembling*
C. S. Lewis's *The Abolition of Man*
Alasdair MacIntyre's *After Virtue*
Marcus Aurelius's *Meditations*
Friedrich Nietzsche's *On the Genealogy of Morality*
Friedrich Nietzsche's *Beyond Good and Evil*
Plato's *Republic*
Plato's *Symposium*
Jean-Jacques Rousseau's *The Social Contract*
Gilbert Ryle's *The Concept of Mind*
Baruch Spinoza's *Ethics*
Sun Tzu's *The Art of War*
Ludwig Wittgenstein's *Philosophical Investigations*

POLITICS

Benedict Anderson's *Imagined Communities*
Aristotle's *Politics*
Bernard Bailyn's *The Ideological Origins of the American Revolution*
Edmund Burke's *Reflections on the Revolution in France*
John C. Calhoun's *A Disquisition on Government*
Ha-Joon Chang's *Kicking Away the Ladder*
Hamid Dabashi's *Iran: A People Interrupted*
Hamid Dabashi's *Theology of Discontent: The Ideological Foundation of the Islamic Revolution in Iran*
Robert Dahl's *Democracy and its Critics*
Robert Dahl's *Who Governs?*
David Brion Davis's *The Problem of Slavery in the Age of Revolution*

Alexis De Tocqueville's *Democracy in America*
James Ferguson's *The Anti-Politics Machine*
Frank Dikotter's *Mao's Great Famine*
Sheila Fitzpatrick's *Everyday Stalinism*
Eric Foner's *Reconstruction: America's Unfinished Revolution, 1863-1877*
Milton Friedman's *Capitalism and Freedom*
Francis Fukuyama's *The End of History and the Last Man*
John Lewis Gaddis's *We Now Know: Rethinking Cold War History*
Ernest Gellner's *Nations and Nationalism*
David Graeber's *Debt: the First 5000 Years*
Antonio Gramsci's *The Prison Notebooks*
Alexander Hamilton, John Jay & James Madison's *The Federalist Papers*
Friedrich Hayek's *The Road to Serfdom*
Christopher Hill's *The World Turned Upside Down*
Thomas Hobbes's *Leviathan*
John A. Hobson's *Imperialism: A Study*
Samuel P. Huntington's *The Clash of Civilizations and the Remaking of World Order*
Tony Judt's *Postwar: A History of Europe Since 1945*
David C. Kang's *China Rising: Peace, Power and Order in East Asia*
Paul Kennedy's *The Rise and Fall of Great Powers*
Robert Keohane's *After Hegemony*
Martin Luther King Jr.'s *Why We Can't Wait*
Henry Kissinger's *World Order: Reflections on the Character of Nations and the Course of History*
John Locke's *Two Treatises of Government*
Niccolò Machiavelli's *The Prince*
Thomas Robert Malthus's *An Essay on the Principle of Population*
Mahmood Mamdani's *Citizen and Subject: Contemporary Africa And The Legacy Of Late Colonialism*
Karl Marx's *Capital*
John Stuart Mill's *On Liberty*
John Stuart Mill's *Utilitarianism*
Hans Morgenthau's *Politics Among Nations*
Thomas Paine's *Common Sense*
Thomas Paine's *Rights of Man*
Thomas Piketty's *Capital in the Twenty-First Century*
Robert D. Putman's *Bowling Alone*
John Rawls's *Theory of Justice*
Jean-Jacques Rousseau's *The Social Contract*
Theda Skocpol's *States and Social Revolutions*
Adam Smith's *The Wealth of Nations*
Sun Tzu's *The Art of War*
Henry David Thoreau's *Civil Disobedience*
Thucydides's *The History of the Peloponnesian War*
Kenneth Waltz's *Theory of International Politics*
Max Weber's *Politics as a Vocation*
Odd Arne Westad's *The Global Cold War: Third World Interventions And The Making Of Our Times*

POSTCOLONIAL STUDIES

Roland Barthes's *Mythologies*
Frantz Fanon's *Black Skin, White Masks*
Homi K. Bhabha's *The Location of Culture*
Gustavo Gutiérrez's *A Theology of Liberation*
Edward Said's *Orientalism*
Gayatri Chakravorty Spivak's *Can the Subaltern Speak?*

PSYCHOLOGY

Gordon Allport's *The Nature of Prejudice*
Alan Baddeley & Graham Hitch's *Aggression: A Social Learning Analysis*
Albert Bandura's *Aggression: A Social Learning Analysis*
Leon Festinger's *A Theory of Cognitive Dissonance*
Sigmund Freud's *The Interpretation of Dreams*
Betty Friedan's *The Feminine Mystique*
Michael R. Gottfredson & Travis Hirschi's *A General Theory of Crime*
Eric Hoffer's *The True Believer: Thoughts on the Nature of Mass Movements*
William James's *Principles of Psychology*
Elizabeth Loftus's *Eyewitness Testimony*
A. H. Maslow's *A Theory of Human Motivation*
Stanley Milgram's *Obedience to Authority*
Steven Pinker's *The Better Angels of Our Nature*
Oliver Sacks's *The Man Who Mistook His Wife For a Hat*
Richard Thaler & Cass Sunstein's *Nudge: Improving Decisions About Health, Wealth and Happiness*
Amos Tversky's *Judgment under Uncertainty: Heuristics and Biases*
Philip Zimbardo's *The Lucifer Effect*

SCIENCE

Rachel Carson's *Silent Spring*
William Cronon's *Nature's Metropolis: Chicago And The Great West*
Alfred W. Crosby's *The Columbian Exchange*
Charles Darwin's *On the Origin of Species*
Richard Dawkin's *The Selfish Gene*
Thomas Kuhn's *The Structure of Scientific Revolutions*
Geoffrey Parker's *Global Crisis: War, Climate Change and Catastrophe in the Seventeenth Century*
Mathis Wackernagel & William Rees's *Our Ecological Footprint*

SOCIOLOGY

Michelle Alexander's *The New Jim Crow: Mass Incarceration in the Age of Colorblindness*
Gordon Allport's *The Nature of Prejudice*
Albert Bandura's *Aggression: A Social Learning Analysis*
Hanna Batatu's *The Old Social Classes And The Revolutionary Movements Of Iraq*
Ha-Joon Chang's *Kicking Away the Ladder*
W. E. B. Du Bois's *The Souls of Black Folk*
Émile Durkheim's *On Suicide*
Frantz Fanon's *Black Skin, White Masks*
Frantz Fanon's *The Wretched of the Earth*
Eric Foner's *Reconstruction: America's Unfinished Revolution, 1863-1877*
Eugene Genovese's *Roll, Jordan, Roll: The World the Slaves Made*
Jack Goldstone's *Revolution and Rebellion in the Early Modern World*
Antonio Gramsci's *The Prison Notebooks*
Richard Herrnstein & Charles A Murray's *The Bell Curve: Intelligence and Class Structure in American Life*
Eric Hoffer's *The True Believer: Thoughts on the Nature of Mass Movements*
Jane Jacobs's *The Death and Life of Great American Cities*
Robert Lucas's *Why Doesn't Capital Flow from Rich to Poor Countries?*
Jay Macleod's *Ain't No Makin' It: Aspirations and Attainment in a Low Income Neighborhood*
Elaine May's *Homeward Bound: American Families in the Cold War Era*
Douglas McGregor's *The Human Side of Enterprise*
C. Wright Mills's *The Sociological Imagination*

Thomas Piketty's *Capital in the Twenty-First Century*
Robert D. Putman's *Bowling Alone*
David Riesman's *The Lonely Crowd: A Study of the Changing American Character*
Edward Said's *Orientalism*
Joan Wallach Scott's *Gender and the Politics of History*
Theda Skocpol's *States and Social Revolutions*
Max Weber's *The Protestant Ethic and the Spirit of Capitalism*

THEOLOGY

Augustine's *Confessions*
Benedict's *Rule of St Benedict*
Gustavo Gutiérrez's *A Theology of Liberation*
Carole Hillenbrand's *The Crusades: Islamic Perspectives*
David Hume's *Dialogues Concerning Natural Religion*
Immanuel Kant's *Religion within the Boundaries of Mere Reason*
Ernst Kantorowicz's *The King's Two Bodies: A Study in Medieval Political Theology*
Søren Kierkegaard's *The Sickness Unto Death*
C. S. Lewis's *The Abolition of Man*
Saba Mahmood's *The Politics of Piety: The Islamic Revival and the Feminist Subject*
Baruch Spinoza's *Ethics*
Keith Thomas's *Religion and the Decline of Magic*

COMING SOON

Chris Argyris's *The Individual and the Organisation*
Seyla Benhabib's *The Rights of Others*
Walter Benjamin's *The Work Of Art in the Age of Mechanical Reproduction*
John Berger's *Ways of Seeing*
Pierre Bourdieu's *Outline of a Theory of Practice*
Mary Douglas's *Purity and Danger*
Roland Dworkin's *Taking Rights Seriously*
James G. March's *Exploration and Exploitation in Organisational Learning*
Ikujiro Nonaka's *A Dynamic Theory of Organizational Knowledge Creation*
Griselda Pollock's *Vision and Difference*
Amartya Sen's *Inequality Re-Examined*
Susan Sontag's *On Photography*
Yasser Tabbaa's *The Transformation of Islamic Art*
Ludwig von Mises's *Theory of Money and Credit*

Macat Disciplines

Access the greatest ideas and thinkers across entire disciplines, including

FEMINISM, GENDER AND QUEER STUDIES

Simone De Beauvoir's
The Second Sex

Michel Foucault's
History of Sexuality

Betty Friedan's
The Feminine Mystique

Saba Mahmood's
*The Politics of Piety:
The Islamic Revival and
the Feminist Subject*

Joan Wallach Scott's
*Gender and the
Politics of History*

Mary Wollstonecraft's
*A Vindication of the
Rights of Woman*

Virginia Woolf's
A Room of One's Own

Judith Butler's
Gender Trouble

Macat analyses are available from all good bookshops and libraries.

Access hundreds of analyses through one, multimedia tool.
Join free for one month **library.macat.com**

Printed in the United States
by Baker & Taylor Publisher Services